1988

PERGAMON INTERNAT
of Science, Technology, Engine
The 1000-volume original pap
education, industrial training and the enjoyment of leisure
Publisher: Robert Maxwell, M.C.

MANAGEMENT AND
INDUSTRIAL STRUCTURE IN JAPAN

Other Titles of Interest

BEALE:
The Manager and the Environment

BLACK:
Public Relations in the 1980s

DAVIES:
Managing and Organizing Multi-national Corporations

DONALD:
Management, Information and Systems, 2nd edn.

DUBRIN:
Fundamentals of Organizational Behaviour, 2nd edn.

EILON:
Aspects of Management, 2nd edn.

EILON:
Management Control, 2nd edn.

GOODMAN & LOVE:
Integrated Project Planning and Management

GOODMAN & LOVE:
Management of Development Projects

HENSHER:
Value of Business Travel Time

HUSSEY:
Introducing Corporate Planning, 2nd edn.

HUSSEY & LANGHAM:
Corporate Planning—The Human Factor

MENDELSOHN:
The Guide to Franchising, 2nd revised edn.

NOLTE:
Fundamentals of Public Relations, 2nd edn.

RIJNSDORP:
Case Studies in Automation Related to Humanization of Work

WEINSTEIN:
Bureaucratic Opposition

A Related Journal

JOURNAL OF ENTERPRISE MANAGEMENT

Aims to improve the quality of management practice by acting as a forum for the exchange of practical and theoretically sound ideas in management decision making and problem solving.
Published three times per year
Free specimen copy available on request

MANAGEMENT AND INDUSTRIAL STRUCTURE IN JAPAN

by

NAOTO SASAKI

Professor of Economics and Industrial Administration,
Sophia University, Tokyo

PERGAMON PRESS

OXFORD · NEW YORK · TORONTO · SYDNEY · PARIS · FRANKFURT

U.K.	Pergamon Press Ltd., Headington Hill Hall, Oxford OX3 0BW, England
U.S.A.	Pergamon Press Inc., Maxwell House, Fairview Park, Elmsford, New York 10523, U.S.A.
CANADA	Pergamon Press Canada Ltd., Suite 104; 150, Consumers Road, Willowdale, Ontario M2J IP9 Canada
AUSTRALIA	Pergamon Press (Aust.) Pty. Ltd., P.O. Box 544, Potts Point, N.S.W. 2011, Australia
FRANCE	Pergamon Press SARL, 24 rue des Ecoles, 75240 Paris, Cedex 05, France
FEDERAL REPUBLIC OF GERMANY	Pergamon Press GmbH, Hammerweg 6, D-6242 Kronberg-Taunus, Federal Republic of Germany

Copyright © 1981 Pergamon Press Ltd.

First edition 1981

Reprinted 1984

British Library Cataloguing in Publication Data
Sasaki, Naoto
Management and industrial structure in Japan
1. Management
2. Associations, institutions, etc. – Japan
I. Title
658′.00952   80–41703
ISBN 0–08–024056–9 (Hardcover)
ISBN 0–08–024057–7 (Flexicover)

Printed in Great Britain by
A. Wheaton & Co. Ltd., Exeter

To my deceased parents

Preface

Already over ten years have passed since I accompanied, as an academic coordinator, a team of thirty Japanese managers to a seminar arranged by the Graduate School of Industrial Administration (GSIA) at Carnegie-Mellon University, Pittsburgh, U.S.A. During the three week stay, students of the school came and asked me to give them a lecture on "Management and the Economy in Japan". This was the first of many such lectures and speeches I have given since in foreign countries.

In the early autumn of that same year I went back to GSIA as a research fellow and, while doing my own research in the field of regulated business behavior, I gave one or two talks to the students. When the one year stay was coming to an end, GSIA members offered me a chance to join them and give a seminar in Europe. This chance opened a gate to Europe to me, and eventually led me to Brussels where I settled down at a newly established institute, the European Institute for Advanced Studies in Management (EIASM) as a visiting fellow.

Looking at my hand to mouth existence, the first dean of EIASM, Professor Richard Van Horn, suggested that I extend the "lecture and speech tour" to Europe to earn a livelihood, and was so kind as to recommend me to various places of management training and education. Thanks to his help and to the growing interest in Japan, gradually I began to be "in demand".

One morning, at the breakfast table in a humble hotel on Rue de la Concorde, an old gentleman talked to me, who turned out to be Dr. Reginald W. Revans of Fondation Industrie-Université. Dr. Revans soon discovered my poverty and kindly introduced me to Dr. Michael Z. Brooke in order to get his help to extend my "tour" to the U.K. Dr. Brooke was at the University of Manchester and was editing a series of international business publications. After a few months he asked me to write a book on Japanese management for his series and so this book was conceived.

In the writing of it I have never forgotten what Dr. Revans told me when I was hesitating whether to return to Japan or not. He said, "Professor Sasaki, Japanese organizations have got so many good things which the Western organizations have not got. If you write a book on Japanese management, go back to your own country, see your organizations with your own eyes and touch them with your own hands."

Finally, after many turns and twists, this book comes into being by courtesy of Mr. Robert Maxwell, Chairman of Pergamon Press Ltd. It is a product of questions raised by my lecture audiences and of my preparations to answer them. However, it is not a book of thorough explanation based on my own research data but one of my own interpretations, based on as many and good existing data as possible, of Management and Industrial Structure in Japan. I do believe, from past experience, that the trade imbalance, for instance, between Europe and Japan has been caused chiefly by "information imbalance". Japanese know very much more about Europe than Europeans know about Japan. There is no comparison. If this book could contribute to filling the gap even a little, I would be very happy.

I gratefully acknowledge the assistance of Dr. Michael Z. Brooke in editing the drafts even though this book no longer forms part of his series. I should also remember the help of Miss Sheila Smith in typing and correcting the drafts. I should like to thank Principal Philip Sadler of Ashridge Management College and Professor Koichi Hamada of Tokyo University for the friendly encouragement they have shown me these ten years.

NAOTO SASAKI

January 1981

Contents

1

The Cultural Background

1.1 The Closed Nature of Japanese Society

As long as management is considered to be the "art" of managing organizations, the practice of management depends on the attributes of the people who form the organization as well as those of the organization itself. It is sometimes difficult to distinguish between the two, but if we do not pay sufficient attention to the difference, we cannot satisfactorily analyze Japanese management. We may misinterpret its unique character.

That it is "closed" is said to be one of the main characteristics of Japanese management, and here the contents of this will be examined. Being "closed" is part of the nature of the Japanese people. Whether they belong to a "closed" organization or not, the Japanese are not socializers. The origin of this may be traced to various features of an ethnic and anthropological nature. For example, geographically Japan is isolated from other countries. In spite of the nearness of Siberia, the Korean Peninsula and China, Japan had had virtually no substantial contact with these countries for many centuries. After the introduction of Buddhism from China through Korea in the 6th century, Japan sent mission after mission to China to learn various things, but with the start and passage of the Tokugawa Shogunate era, she gradually developed a policy of seclusion from other countries, and finally in 1639, officially announced a complete self-imposed seclusion. Since the Meiji Restoration in 1868, when the country was opened to foreigners, up to very recent years she pursued the progress of the "civilized countries" in the West. Accordingly, it may be accurate to say that Japan was not paying much attention to her neighbouring countries for almost four hundred years. Linguistically and culturally, the Japanese are a homogeneous race and very defensive against entrants from the outside, greatly because they live on irrigation farming, sharing the water supply only among themselves. Of the possible reasons for this the most distinctive is that Japan has never been invaded by a different ethnic group at any time in her whole history. Of course there was the United States occupation for some time after World War II, but this experience did not present itself on a sufficiently wide scale to influence greatly the basic outlook of the people. Thus, in addition to the geographical isolation, Japan has formed, as mentioned above, a culturally isolated island through promoting Westernization with a resultant detachment from Asia while strengthening her characteristics as a racially homogeneous society of a sort rarely found in the history of the world.

Foreigners are not the only victims of this characteristic. All Japanese seem to possess, at least potentially, what may be called "group cohesiveness". They can at any time identify themselves with an organization to which they belong, even if temporarily, and at the same time show a stubborn barrier against other organizations. This "closed" behaviour sometimes takes an offensive form. It has been noticed that students from two different high schools from the same prefecture fight with each other over minor matters. However, when confronted with students from another prefecture they quite easily join forces and form a new group showing a broader enclosure. As a result, an even bigger conflict may take place between students from different prefectures. And the broadest unit of such groups is Japan. This notion does not extend, however, to the ambiguously bordered entity "the society". Namely the Japanese people are lacking in the feeling of being "members of the public", which is often pointed out to be the reason for low public moral in Japan. As such the closed nature of Japanese firms is intrinsic to the Japanese people in the first place. However, this national characteristic must be clearly distinguished from the type of enclosure which firms develop as a system.

The lack of sociability on the part of the Japanese people often invites misunderstandings. For example, the Japanese are not good when talking to others at looking them straight in the face. When they feel shy, they steal a glance "from the corner of their eyes", to use a Western expression, and it is often wrongly assumed that an insult is intended. In Japan it is considered as a virtue to hide one's own feelings, whereas in Western countries the lack of frank expression creates problems in human relations.

Many of the troubles which Japanese firms have created abroad can in fact be traced to this individual trait.

What would then be the factor contributing to the creation of the character in the Japanese firms as a system? The biggest factor may well be the life-time employment system. Japanese employees may be by nature loyal to the firm that employs them. On the other hand loyalty can be nurtured as it is usually the case that the longer a person stays with an organization, the more loyal he becomes. Therefore, under the life-time employment system, loyalty is strengthened as one's position rises within an organization. The seniority system, supporting lifetime employment from inside, and the wage system based on seniority are other "closed" systems found in Japanese firms. The rapid growth of the Japanese economy in the 1960s caused labour shortages in some sectors of the society but did not leave behind much labour mobility if compared internationally as Table 1.1 shows.

TABLE 1.1 *How many times have you changed jobs?*

(%)

	Japan	U.S.A.	U.K.	F.R. Germany	India
Never	71.5	23.0	41.4	56.1	85.2
Once	14.8	17.9	23.8	24.9	9.0
Twice	5.4	18.2	14.6	12.5	2.4
Three times	2.2	13.3	7.7	3.6	0.4
Four or more times	1.3	27.0	12.2	1.8	0.7
No answer	4.9	0.7	0.3	1.1	2.3

Source: *The Japanese Youth*, The Prime Minister's Office, Tokyo, 1978.
Note: The samples are youth in each country whose ages are 18 to 24 inclusive.

Those in higher positions in an organization are usually older and better paid. This system almost completely eliminates the possibility of labour mobility among firms; it is extremely difficult to find a job in other firms with similar, let alone improved, terms and conditions. It is often said that Japanese youth have changed towards more meritocracy. But if we make another international comparison, as is shown in Table 1.2, they still have a preference for the seniority system. In this table we should pay more attention to the fourth item than to the first three as it is taken to be a more honest expression of their feelings. The seniority system is too deeply rooted in the heart of the Japanese people to disappear overnight.

TABLE 1.2 *How would you like promotions and salary increases to be decided?*

(%)

	Japan	U.S.A.	U.K.	F.R. Germany	Sweden
Only by seniority	10.2	2.1	3.2	3.7	14.2
Mainly by seniority but performance also considered	36.0	14.0	12.4	14.3	27.6
Mainly by performance but seniority also considered	25.8	44.9	40.8	39.2	30.5
Only by performance	6.5	34.3	35.5	39.0	12.6

Source: *The Japanese Youth*, The Prime Minister's Office, Tokyo, 1978.
Note: The samples are youth in each country whose ages are 18 to 24 inclusive.

When these closed systems are combined with the intrinsic closed-mindedness and group cohesiveness of the Japanese people themselves, they begin to show a total situation which may be extremely strong and exclusive. When they are further amplified by unsociability and un-friendly looks, they may give an impression of a rock hard coldness towards outsiders. It is here that the concepts of *Uchi*, the insides of one's world, and *Soto*, the outside, emerge.[1]*

1.2 Social Norms

The closed-mindedness and the group cohesiveness mentioned above are often described as "collectivism". But they should be considered as

* Superior numbers refer to the "Notes" at the end of each chapter.

unconscious social norms rather than as rationally designed ideologies. Group decision-making based on consensus, for example, is a product of this norm. As the community, *Uchi*, is formed within an originally homogeneous society each member naturally wishes to obtain agreement from other members about his own activities and when he gains the agreement, he feels at ease, and in turn shows interest in the activities of others. Consensus by all the members is therefore necessary, to make an extreme statement, for every activity in an organization. Accordingly it is likely to be a norm that members of an organization discuss their intentions with each other, on the basis of existing information. After completion of a particular activity, they report the results to one another. Through this process of sharing information, the parties confirm that they are members of the same organization. The complexity involved in exchanging information is multiplied as the number of members grows. Japanese firms spend a great amount of energy in developing a consensus. The criticism that Japanese managers in their foreign subsidiaries are over-concerned about their head office's reactions is often heard. In fact, however, this concern is usually part of the consensus forming process between the head office and the subsidiaries. Attention should be paid to the fact that this can happen regardless of the degree of authority delegated to the subsidiaries. This can make the system appear to be a centralized one.

To express the situation differently, in the homogeneous society of Japan it is vital for each member to keep harmony with other members of his organization. It may not be too extreme to say that cutting an over-conspicuous figure in a Japanese organization is regarded as a sin. For example, if a business manager becomes famous as an economist in the outside world, or *Soto*, he will have only a narrow chance of being promoted to the top. Quite often Japanese management style is characterized as familyism. But in a family to be conspicuous is not a sin. The familyism of Japanese organizations, therefore, should not be exaggerated. It would not be unreasonable to say that it is partly a product of egalitarianism backed with jealousy. As a matter of fact, this egalitarianism has been advancing also in terms of economic equality. Table 1.3 shows that the gaps in the lifetime income among primary and/or middle school graduates, high school graduates, and university graduates are getting smaller. This is proved internationally, too. According to an OECD report, the income gap between the rich and the poor is the smallest in

TABLE 1.3 *Differences of lifetime income by school careers*

(index)

	Primary and middle school graduates	High school graduates	University graduates
1965	57.7	70.2	100.0
1977	74.5	75.6	100.0

Source: *Trend of Life and Consciousness of the Japanese*, The Economic Planning Agency, Tokyo, 1979.

TABLE 1.4 *Consciousness of the people of belonging to income class*

(%)

Classes	1962	1975	1978
Upper upper	0.4	0.8	0.9
Lower upper	2.1	3.0	4.8
Upper middle	35.0	43.4	49.3
Lower middle	38.2	35.3	31.7
Upper lower	12.2	7.4	7.0
Lower lower	3.7	2.4	2.0

Source: *Trend of Life and Consciousness of the Japanese*, The Economic Planning Agency, Tokyo, 1979.

Japan among the OECD countries, and the income equalization is most advanced.[2] Though there may not be much difference among those countries, as Table 1.4 shows, a great majority of the people in Japan consider themselves to be "middle class".

In some respects, however, true familyism does exist in Japan. For instance, from time to time Japanese managers abroad receive publicity for the way in which they work with local workers and mix with them. This is not at all unusual in Japan where plant managers and supervisors concern themselves with the private affairs of their workers or subordinates. Frequently managers invite their staff for a drink after work, and it is not rare when a manager is transferred to another plant or office that his workers and subordinates come to the house to help with the packing, cleaning and other activities, and on the day he leaves they line up at the railway station to see him off. Such a scene would not be understood in Western society. What may be considered as an invasion of privacy in the West is accepted in Japan as consideration for subordinates.

An extreme example of this is found in the case of Idemitsu Petroleum. There they have neither time recorders nor a retirement age. According to Mr. Idemitsu, a past president of the company, "We do not fire employees, no matter what bad ways they may have. Who would fire his children? As we do not let them quit, we do not have to have a retirement age. If an employee gets married, we will pay his wife 60% of his wage or salary, because we think she has become a member of our family. And we do not give any sanction or penalty. Let a child think over his failure, then he will learn from it."[3] As a matter of fact, still at present in progress of so-called "Westernization" more than 70% of Japanese youth think it better to live with their parents when the latter gets old. This figure is contrasted with 23% of the youth in the United States and 13% in F.R. Germany.[4]

What is to be noted, concerning this familyism, is that the father or the leader should not have or even wish to have authoritative power. The leader should be a man who "takes care" of those around him.[5] This has much to do with group leadership not only in the business organization but also in government. It is the inheritance of a long political tradition, which can be traced back to the thirteenth century when the political body already had a power-sharing system. In the Tokugawa era, prior to the Meiji Restoration, this sytem of group leadership was developed to its full extreme. Again, after the Restoration, the new leaders continued its practice. In Japan "unlike the situation in most countries undergoing rapid change, there was never any one dictatorial leader, nor did any person ever attempt to gain such powers".[6]

In this sytem authority based on seniority coexists, at first sight strangely, with the egalitarianism which lets members of an organization say: "Let's all share work together, enjoy and suffer together, as we are members of the same family".

1.3 A Plywood of Traditional and Imported Systems

The Japanese society is "mysterious" to foreigners and quite often confuses them to the point that they use descriptive phrases such as the "Face of the East behind a Western Mask"[7] or, in the extreme case, "Schizophrenic Superstate".[8] Perhaps the following quotation seems to be the most comprehensive of the impressions of foreigners.

> "Japan is a society of great complexity and subtlety. The best word I can think of to describe it is that it is a mosaic society, in the sense that it is composed of numerous colourful pieces all of which together form, in some mysterious way, a pattern. If I may be permitted to play on words, it is the least Mosaic of all societies, participating hardly at all in the great stream of history which comes down from Mt. Sinai—until the last one hundred years".[9]

What should be kept in mind is that in the course of those 100 years of modernization, accompanied by an extremely rapid economic growth, the Japanese people have always looked to Western society as a model. Prior to World War II, everything was geared towards European methods. The philosophy and technology taught in the schools and universities were almost exclusively those of Europe. Songs taught in primary schools were usually from Britain or Germany. After World War II, the United States took the place of Europe as a favourite subject for investigation and admiration on the part of the Japanese people. Hence, although Japan had some involvement with South-east Asian countries in the form of the Greater East Asia Co-Prosperity Sphere, such schemes were kept outside the normal modernization process. Much earlier, after the Meiji Restoration in 1868, she hastily started adopting Western or European technologies, the civil service system, and educational system—"a craze for Westernization",[10] as it has been called.

But in this process, the Japanese have naturally followed a principle called *Wa Kon Yoh Sai* which means "Japanese Spirit and Western Technology". This westernization has been so extensive in all aspects of life in Japan that the behaviour of businesses, for instance, looks much the same as that in the West. This may give the impression that the behaviour is thought out in the way it would be in the West, too. But this is not the case. The norms of business conduct form a pseudo-amalgamation or, more precisely, a plywood of two different sets of norms—the Japanese and the Western. Let us denote them N_j (Japanese norms) and N_w (Western norms) respectively and classify situations where they function differently thus:

Situation 1: $N_j = N_w$
This situation comes about when the environment is stable and routine dominates the daily business. Here it is quite natural if foreigners think that the style of management in Japan is Westernized.

Situation 2: $N_j \neq N_w$
When uncertainty grows larger in the environment these two start to separate or quite often abruptly split. Here managers behave Japanese at a moment and may behave Western at the next.

Situation 3: $N_j > N_w$
A crisis or a difficulty can change in a flash a Westernized Japanese to a pure Japanese, who sets back and clings to N_j.

Notes

1. See C. Nakane, *Japanese Society*, Penguin Books, 1973, Ch. 1.
2. See M. Sawyer, *Income Distribution in OECD Countries*, OECD, Paris, 1976.
3. *The Evening Tokyo*, Tokyo, 6 December 1973.
4. See *White Paper on the Youth*, The Prime Minister's Office, Tokyo, 1978, p. 20.
5. This interpretation is indebted to the remark of Mr. S. Yamamoto in *The Weekly Asahi*, Tokyo, 27 May 1977, p. 136.
6. E. O. Reischauer, *The Japanese*, Harvard University Press, 1977, p. 239.
7. *The Times*, London, 19 June 1972, p. 12.
8. *Nova*, London, April 1972. (The cover story, "Japan—the schizophrenic superstate" by Irma Kurtz.)
9. K. E. Boulding, *A Primer on Social Dynamics*, The Free Press, New York, 1970, p. 133.
10. E. O. Reischauer, *Japan*, Charles E. Tuttle Co., Tokyo, 1974, p. 141.

2

The Economic Background

2.1 The Industrial Structure

Industrial Groups

These may roughly be classified into two categories. One is a group in which member companies have a close relationship with financing institutions whose core is a main bank. The other is independent of particular financial ties, and does not have a main bank. Table 2.1 shows a few examples.

Mitsubishi Electric, Mitsui Toatsu Chemicals and Sumitomo Cement are examples of companies with close financial relations with their group's main bank. Most of the bank loans for these companies are financed by the Mitsubishi, Mitsui and Sumitomo banks respectively. Hitachi is an example of a company that does not depend on a particular bank. It would be realistic to think of Hitachi as a financially independent company, though it participates in the president's meetings of both the Fuji and the Sanwa Bank Groups.

Before the merger of Nissan and Prince into the new Nissan Motors, the main bank of the former was Fuji and that of the latter was Sumitomo. Since the merger, therefore, Nissan Motors has two main banks. Like Hitachi, however, this company should be taken to be independent. Toyota has a very sound financial position and is run on internally generated funds. In the case of Sony, though it seems to have a strong financial tie with the Mitsui Bank, it is not considered a member company of the Mitsui Group. The tie is said to be based on the personal relationship between past presidents of the two concerns.

Among the six financially linked groups the Mitsui, the Mitsubishi

TABLE 2.1 *Patterns of bank loan*

1976 (million yen)

Bank \ Mfg. Co.	Mitsui Bank and Mitsui Trust & Banking	Mitsubishi Bank and Mitsubishi Trust & Banking	Sumitomo Bank and Sumitomo Trust & Banking	Fuji Bank and Yasuda Trust & Banking	Sanwa Bank and Toyo Trust & Banking	Dai-Ichi Kangyo Bank
Hitachi	12,243	19,040	19,730	46,821	45,260	45,202
Mitsubishi Electric	26,456	85,562	10,340	4,986	3,254	26,524
Sony	9,750	1,900	—	1,900	1,000	1,900
Toyota Motor (1971)*	1,200	500	100	500	1,000	100
Nissan Motor	7,999	20,127	42,191	67,243	22,106	11,530
Mitsui Toatsu Chemicals	59,155	4,461	130	—	562	6,350
Sumitomo Cement	4,125	1,300	21,805	—	613	—

* Since 1972 Toyota has not had loans from these banks.
Source: Kigyo Keiretsu Soran, Toyo Keizai, Tokyo, 1978.

and the Sumitomo groups have stronger ties than the other three. These three were Zaibatsu groups, each of which was owned by a holding company before World War II, but which were dissolved by the American Occupation Authorities afterwards. So now they are not under the control of a holding company. What then is, for example, the Mitsui Group?

TABLE 2.2 *Holding of shares of Mitsui Toatsu Chemicals*

(a) Substantial share-holders in Mitsui Toatsu Chemicals.

Mitsui Mutual Life Insurance	3.16
Mitsui Bank	2.91
Taisho Marine and Fire Insurance	2.35
Mitsui Trust and Banking	2.28
Mitsui and Co.	2.27
Mitsui Real Estate Development	0.49
Mitsui Petrochemical Industries	0.46
Mitsui Construction	0.23
Mitsui Shipbuilding and Engineering	0.20
Mitsui Warehouse	0.18
Total	14.53%

Loans to Mitsui Toatsu Chemicals from Mitsui Bank, Mitsui Trust and Banking, Taisho Marine and Fire Insurance and Mitsui Mutual Life Insurance amount to 27.23% of all loans.

(b) Percentage of the stocks of *Nimoku-kai* companies owned by Mitsui Toatsu Chemicals.

Mitsui Bank	0.59
Mitsui Trust and Banking	0.72
Taisho Marine and Fire Insurance	0.51
Mitsui Mining	0.42
Mitsui Construction	0.53
Mitsui Petrochemical Industries	2.47
Tokyo Shibaura Electric	0.02
Mitsui and Co.	0.17

Source: *Kigyo Keiretsu Soran*, Toyo Keizai, Tokyo, 1974.

The companies belonging to the Mitsui Group are those which have a close relationship with the financing institutions which centre around Mitsui Bank, conduct large economic transactions with the trading company of the same name, and are members of the Group's policy-making organ, the *Nimoku-kai* ("the Second Thursday Conference"). This is composed of the presidents of the participating companies.[1] The core of the Group is the Mitsui Bank and the trading company, Mitsui & Co., and the Group member companies are holding their shares mutually and have cross membership in their boards of directors. Table 2.2 shows the cross holdings of shares of Mitsui Toatsu Chemicals, a member company of the Mitsui Group. Mitsui Bank and Mitsui & Co. are, of course, financially tied as is shown in Table 2.3. These characteristics of the Mitsui Group are also true of the other two groups, the Mitsubishi and the Sumitomo. Member companies of these three groups are listed below.

The Mitsui Group
The twenty-three companies that participate in the presidents' council are:

Mitsui Bank
Mitsui Trust and Banking
Mitsui Mutual Life Insurance
Taisho Marine and Fire Insurance
Mitsui Mining
Hokkaido Colliery and Steamship
Mitsui Construction
Sanki Engineering
Nippon Flour Mills
Toray Industries
Oji Paper
Mitsui Toatsu Chemicals
Mitsui Petrochemical Industries
Japan Steel Works
Mitsui Mining and Smelting
Mitsui Shipbuilding and Engineering
Mitsui and Co.
Mitsukoshi Department Store
Mitsui Real Estate Development
Mitsui O.S.K. Lines

TABLE 2.3 *Financial relationships between banks and trading companies*

(Amount of loans) 1978
(million yen)

Bank \ Trading Co.	Mitsui	Mitsubishi	Sumitomo	Fuji	Sanwa	Dai-Ichi Kangyo
Mitsui and Co.	260,768	85,804	111,813	181,751	87,232	48,588
Mitsubishi Co.	19,400	310,920	43,731	34,134	104,121	92,778
Sumitomo Shoji	9,896	33,895	143,598	770	3,575	370
Maubeni Co.	19,420	82,441	50,819	182,117	46,974	5,811
Nissho-Iwai Co.	24,146	27,066	14,221	9,722	113,913	72,621

Source: Kigyo Keiretsu Soran, Toyo Keizai, Tokyo, 1978.

Mitsui Warehouse
Tokyo Shibaura Electric
Toyota Motor

(The last two companies have a certain independence from the Mitsui Group, but are represented on the presidents' council.)

The Mitsubishi Group
The twenty-eight companies that participate in the presidents' council are:

Mitsubishi Bank
Mitsubishi Mutual Trust and Banking
Meiji Mutual Life Insurance
Tokio Marine and Fire Insurance
Kirin Beer Brewery
Mitsubishi Rayon
Mitsubishi Paper Mills
Mitsubishi Chemical Industries
Mitsubishi Gas-Chemical
Mitsubishi Petrochemical
Mitsubishi Plastics Industries
Mitsubishi Oil
Asahi Glass
Mitsubishi Mining and Cement
Mitsubishi Steel Manufacturing
Mitsubishi Metal Corporation
Mitsubishi Kakoki Kaisha
Mitsubishi Electric Corporation
Mitsubishi Heavy Industries
Nippon Kogaku (Nikon)
Mitsubishi Corporation
Mitsubishi Estate
Nippon Yusen
Mitsubishi Warehouse and Transportation
Mitsubishi Monsanto Chemical
Mitsubishi Motors Corporation
Mitsubishi Aluminum
Mitsubishi Construction

The Sumitomo Group

The twenty-one companies that participate in the presidents' council are:

Sumitomo Bank
Sumitomo Trust and Banking
Sumitomo Mutual Life Insurance
Sumitomo Marine and Fire Insurance
Sumitomo Coal Mining
Sumitomo Chemical
Nippon Sheet Glass
Sumitomo Cement
Sumitomo Metal Industries
Sumitomo Metal Mining
Sumitomo Electric Industries
Sumitomo Heavy Industries
Nippon Electric
Sumitomo Shoji Kaisha
Sumitomo Realty and Development
Sumitomo Warehouse
Sumitomo Construction
Sumitomo Light Metal
Sumitomo Bakelite
Sumitomo Forestry
Sumitomo Aluminium Refinery

The other three financially allied groups are the Fuji Bank Group (Fuyo Group) which has 29 member companies, the Sanwa Bank Group having 35 member companies, and the Dai-Ichi Kangyo Bank (DKB) Group with more than 30 companies. The core of each of these three groups is also a bank and a trading company and they have almost the same array of industries as that of the former three, but have a relatively loose tie.

As we have seen, each of these six industrial groups includes every industry. This is best described by a slogan the Mitsubishi Group used to have: "From noodle to atomic power". This policy is called "one-set-ism". Therefore, in one industry in Japan, let's say the chemical industry, there are at least six competing chemical companies. It could be said that the

Japanese economy includes six subeconomies which are miniatures of the whole. This kind of phenomenon may be rooted somewhere in the Japanese mentality. For example, every private university in Japan wishes to have facilities that range from kindergarten to graduate school, and is inclined to "campus nationalism" concerning the teaching staff. Group nationalism of the industrial groups is often found especially in the development of new big projects, which will be described later in Chapter 5, as well as in the groups' roles and functions in the economy.

In addition to these financially allied groups gathering around the main bank and the trading company, there are ten or so independent manufacturers' groups comprised of numerous member companies. Some of them are:

Nippon Steel Group
Hitachi Group
Tokyo Shibaura (Toshiba) Electric Group
Ishikawajima-Harima Heavy Industries (IHI) Group
Nissan Group
Toyota Group
Matsushita Group
Tokyu Group

Dual Structure

The rapid growth of the Japanese economy has brought about uneven growth between two sectors. One is that of big businesses, and the other is that of small and medium enterprises. The size distribution of manufacturers in Japan, shown by Table 2.4, clearly indicates that almost 98% of the manufacturing companies have less than 100 employees. This distribution is said to have remained unchanged during the last twenty or more years, and is peculiar to Japan among the highly advanced industrialized countries as is shown by Table 2.5.

What is important existing along with this distribution is the productivity gap between the numerous small manufacturing companies and a few big ones. This gap naturally leads to another gap, that of wages. Table 2.6 and 2.7 show these two gaps. The wage gap by size of establishment is again peculiar to Japan as we can see in Table 2.8.

TABLE 2.4 *The size of establishments*

(%)

Number of employees	1966	1967	1968	1969	1970	1971	1972	1973	1974
1–9	72.8	72.7	72.6	73.5	73.4	73.3	74.4	74.4	75.1
10–19	13.7	14.0	14.0	13.7	13.6	13.6	13.2	13.2	12.7
20–99	11.3	11.0	11.0	10.5	10.6	10.7	10.2	10.1	10.0
100–299	1.6	1.7	1.8	1.7	1.8	1.8	1.6	1.7	1.6
300–999	0.5	0.5	0.5	0.5	0.5	0.5	0.5	0.5	0.5
1,000 and over	0.1	0.1	0.1	0.1	0.1	0.1	0.1	0.1	0.1
Total number of establishment	594,832	598,958	602,388	646,926	652,931	643,552	702,586	708,447	696,795

Source: White Paper on Small and Medium Enterprises, Small and Medium Enterprises Agency, Tokyo, 1976.
Table 2.4 shows the size distribution not of companies but of establishments of manufacturing companies. The number of companies, however, exceeds 90% of that of establishments in each class, and, therefore, the proportions would not have to be modified greatly even if we used the number of companies. Company numbers of the smallest two classes are not obtainable in the Government statistics.

TABLE 2.5 *Employment structure in manufacturing in four countries*

Size of establishment	U.S.A. (1958)		Japan (1964)		F.R. Germany (1961)		U.K. (1958)	
	thousand	%	thousand	%	thousand	%	thousand	%
1–49 employees	2,645.3	(17.2)	4,108	(41.5)	2,757.6	(29.0)	897	(11.7)
50–99	1,512.8	(9.8)	1,115	(11.3)	676.8	(7.1)	658	(8.6)
100–499	4,647.3	(30.2)	2,183	(22.0)	2,260.2	(23.8)	2,428	(31.6)
500–999	1,893.3	(12.3)	808	(8.2)	1,007.0	(10.6)	1,043	(14.6)
1,000 and over	4,695.1	(30.5)	1,687	(17.0)	2,806.0	(29.5)	2,654	(34.5)
Total	15,393.8	(100.0)	9,901	(100.0)	9,507.6	(100.0)	7,680	(100.0)

Source: Miyohei Shinohara, *Structural Changes in Japan's Economic Development*, Kinokuniya Bookstore, Tokyo, 1970 (quoted with the permission of the author).

TABLE 2.6 *Productivity differentials by size of enterprise*

Number of employees	1966	1967	1968	1969	1970	1971	1972	1973
1–3	23	21	22	22	22	23	34	34
4–9	35	34	35	34	36	36		
10–19	46	44	45	44	46	47	48	52
20–99	53	52	54	53	54	55	54	56
100–299	68	68	69	66	67	70	69	71
300 and over	100	100	100	100	100	100	100	100

Source: *White Paper on Small and Medium Enterprises*, Small and Medium Enterprises Agency, Tokyo, 1976.

TABLE 2.7 *Wage differentials by size of enterprise*

Number of employees	1966	1967	1968	1969	1970	1971	1972	1973
1–3	12	12	12	16	13	13	38	39
4–9	44	45	46	47	47	47		
10–19	61	62	63	64	63	62	61	63
20–99	69	71	71	71	70	71	68	69
100–299	78	78	78	77	77	77	78	77
300 and over	100	100	100	100	100	100	100	100

Source: *White Paper on Small and Medium Enterprises*, Small and Medium Enterprises Agency, Tokyo, 1976.

If we combine these findings with Table 2.9, we may reason that roughly 70% of the workers working for small and medium companies get only 60% or less wage of that of workers working for big businesses.

What we have here is evidence of the so-called "dual structure" in the Japanese economy. A few big businesses with high productivity and high wages and numerous small and medium companies with low productivity and low wages coexist. The latter have been left behind by the progress of the former, and have had less advantages in the way of financial supplies and government assistance.

TABLE 2.8 *Wage differentials in manufacturing in four advanced countries*

	Japan (1976)	U.K. (1954)	U.S.A. (1967)	F.R. Germany (1967)
1,000 and over	100.0	100.0	100.0	100.0
500–999	85.8	89.3	81.3	90.5
100–499	74.0	86.8	75.0	84.1
50–99	62.3	80.9	72.5	77.1
10–49	59.3	79.9	73.8	69.7

Source: *Rodo Tokei Yoran* (Handbook of Labour Statistics), Ministry of Labour, Tokyo, 1979.
Note: In 1960 these indexes in Japan were 100.0, 78.7, 64.4, 55.0, and 48.5, though in other countries they were almost the same as in this table.

This dual structure is not only a structure with productivity and wage differences but also that with control. For those numerous small and medium companies are mostly related subcontractors of big businesses, and they are fixed in the layers of subcontracting structure which has a hierarchy of parts suppliers.

Table 2.10 is a list of related companies or subcontractors of Mitsui Toatsu Chemicals, where we find that the companies in the list are under the personnel as well as the financial control of the parent company. For instance, in the case of Toyo Gas Chemical, 50% of the stocks are owned by the parent company, Mitsui Toatsu Chemicals, and out of 8 directors, 5 are from the parent company. If we take into account possible loans Toyo Gas Chemical may have borrowed from the parent company, the financial control would be equivalent to a majority ownership.

A typical pattern of this kind of pyramidal structure of subcontracting is found in the automobile industry. "Internal production ratio"—a ratio that products to be used or assembled for a car are produced internally within the parent company—of Japanese automobile manufacturers is between 30 to 35%. In other words, from 65 to 70% of the products or parts used to make a complete car are produced by subcontractors. At times some marginal subcontractors are treated as if they were shock absorbers of recession. But by and large, as the quality of the finished product depends on the parts supplied by the subcontractors, parent

TABLE 2.9 *Distribution of workers by size of company*

(%)

Number of workers per establishment	1966	1967	1968	1969	1970	1971	1972	1973	1974	1975
1–9	16.6	16.4	16.6	16.6	16.4	16.3	17.4	17.4	17.7	19.1
10–19	11.2	11.2	11.1	11.3	10.8	10.8	11.2	11.1	10.9	11.4
20–99	26.2	25.5	24.9	24.5	24.4	24.8	25.0	24.6	24.8	25.2
100–299	15.8	15.7	15.9	15.7	15.9	16.1	15.9	16.0	15.7	15.1
300–999	14.2	14.5	14.6	14.7	15.0	14.9	14.8	14.8	14.6	13.7
1,000 and over	11.2	16.7	17.4	17.5	17.5	17.1	16.0	16.2	16.2	15.6
1–299	69.7	68.8	68.8	67.9	67.5	67.9	69.5	69.0	69.2	70.7
300 and over	30.3	31.2	32.0	32.1	32.5	32.1	30.5	31.0	30.8	29.3
Total	100.0	100.0	100.0	100.0	100.0	100.0	100.0	100.0	100.0	100.0

Source: White Paper on Small and Medium Enterprises, Small and Medium Enterprises Agency, Tokyo, 1976.

TABLE 2.10 *Related companies of Mitsui Toatsu Chemicals (MTC)*

Company name	Ratio of the stocks owned by MTC	Employees number	Number of directors (*)
Toyo Engineering	60	1,198	16 (13)
Kanto N. G. Kaihatsu	85	187	6 (5)
Toyo Gas Chemical	50	310	8 (5)
Osaka Petrochemical	50	274	16 (8)
Nippon A. Aluminum	75	55	6 (4)
Mitsui Toatsu Warehouse	98.6	26	5 (5)
Shintomi Transport	99.3	110	3 (2)
Orient	100	266	4 (4)
Toyo Fibre Glass	100	88	3 (3)
Senhoku Hydrogen	50	13	8 (4)
Anjo Plastic	50	65	6 (5)
Sansei Chemical	93	145	10 (9)
Toyo Kosan	100	53	6 (6)
Toyo Service	100	20	4 (4)
Sanshin Sangyo	83	52	9 (8)
Toyo Sports	50	13	5 (4)
Toyo Colouring	100	35	4 (4)
Other 40 companies			

(*) Numbers in the parentheses are the numbers of directors sent from MTC on a mission.
Source: Kigyo Keiretsu Soran, Toyo Keizai, Tokyo, 1974.

companies take good care of them. For example, Toyota subcontractors have an association, called the *Kyoho-kai*, having 133 member companies in which they confront and solve their problems jointly.

The point is that small and medium companies as subcontractors usually maintain continuous and exclusive relations with their parent companies and they became, as a result, substantial members of the industrial groups. To calculate the weight of these industrial groups in the Japanese economy depends on to what degree we should take the controllability of them into consideration. We have a few attempts of the estimation of variety. One is by Toyo Keizai where they estimate sales shares of the big six, Mitsui, Mitsubishi, Sumitomo, Sanwa, Fuji and DKB groups in 1977 are 2.77%, 2.82%, 1.67%, 2.72%, 2.73% and 4.31% respectively. In this case they took into account only those member companies attending the presidents' meeting. K. Bieda[2] and the Dodwell[3] put heavier weight upon them. According to the latter, their sales shares, in the same order, are 10.0% and 13.2%, 10.1%, 8.5%, 8.5% and 9.1%. This line of reasoning would give us a valid conclusion that the existence of ten or so industrial groups, including the big six, accounts for about half of the total economy. More details will be discussed later in Chapter 5.

2.2 Finance: "Over Borrowing"

The high rate of growth of the Japanese economy has been achieved by a high rate of investment especially by private companies. This high investment rate has been supported by personal savings as is shown in Table 2.11.

There are theories about the reason why the savings ratio in Japan has been so high. The major reasons suggested are as follows:

(1) Japanese companies usually pay bonuses twice a year—one in June and the other in December—amounting to more than three months wages and salaries. These bonuses increase the propensity to save.

(2) As the social security system, especially after the retirement age, is poor and unreliable, people have to save for their future even when their income is not sufficient to do so.

(3) Under the seniority wage and salary system the older get more pay with less expenses because, for example, their children have finished education. This would increase their savings ratio.

The immaturity of the securities market in Japan and the aversion of the Japanese people to speculation, possibly as a result of Confucian influence, have directed savings to the commercial banks. The manufacturing companies have not had their own funds sufficient for growth, so they have been financed by the banks.

But the banks themselves have not had sufficient sources. Sometimes they have lent more than is permitted by the law on reserve ratios and this deficit has been filled by money borrowed from the Bank of Japan.

As a result the financial position of Japanese companies on the average is quite weak and "unsound" and could be described as "over borrowing". Table 2.12 shows this situation. In addition to this the reported fact that

TABLE 2.11 *Propensity to save by country*

	1965	1966	1967	1968	1969	1970	1971	1972	1973	1974	1975	1976	1977
Japan	17.9	16.9	17.6	18.9	18.7	18.1	17.5	18.0	20.5	23.7	22.5	22.4	21.2
U.S.A.	6.6	6.6	7.7	6.6	5.7	7.6	7.9	6.3	8.0	7.5	7.9	5.9	5.3
England	6.3	6.6	5.8	5.1	5.4	6.1	5.7	7.4	7.9	10.0	10.9	10.6	10.1
F.R. Germany	16.8	15.7	15.6	17.0	15.5	17.9	17.0	15.3	13.5	13.8	14.1	12.3	12.1
France	11.4	11.3	11.8	11.4	10.4	12.6	13.1	13.2	13.7	13.6	14.9	12.1	13.2

Source: Kokusai Hikaku Tokei (International Comparative Statistics), Bank of Japan, Tokyo, 1979.
Note: Propensity to save is the ratio of the savings by household to the disposable income of household.

TABLE 2.12 *Trend of debt-equity ratio*

(%)

	1968	1971	1974	1977
Debt	83.1	84.2	85.7	85.9
Equity	16.9	15.8	14.3	14.1

Source: *Zaisei Kinyu Tokei Geppo* (Monthly Report of Fiscal and Financial Statistics), Ministry of Finance, Tokyo, 1978.

the overwhelming proportion of professional managers as against owner-managers makes the economy even more fragile.[4] This was 20% in 1900, 50% in 1925 and is at present as high as 90%. But it is also true that in the period of growth the companies preferred borrowed funds to increasing their capital.

The cost of this high proportion of loan capital can be appreciated when it is realized that the rate of interest for the borrowed money on net profits reaches almost 5% in Japan, while it is less than 1% in U.S.A. and the U.K. If we compare this cost in Japanese companies in 1965 with labour costs in Nissan Motor, for instance, the proportions were 90.2 (cost of money) versus 100 (labour cost), and in the case of Matsushita Electric they were 50.5 versus 100, while the same proportions for General Motors, Volkswagen and General Electric were 0.3, 1.4, and 0.4 respectively.[5]

Japanese companies also have a great deal of intercorporate credit. This credit has been one wheel driving to fast growth. Another has been money borrowed from financial institutions (commercial banks, governmental banks and small finance companies and cooperatives).

2.3 Technology: Process Innovation

Before the War Japanese products were said to be "copied" and "cheap and bad". But afterwards, especially in recent years, the quality has been greatly improved, and they are regarded now as "cheap and good", though still quite often lacking in originality. Table 2.13 shows the balance of Japan's technology trade and its comparison with other industrial

TABLE 2.13 Balance of Japan's technology trade

(million dollars)

	Japan			U.S.A.			U.K.			France			F.R. Germany		
	Exports (A)	Imports (B)	A/B	Exports (A)	Imports (B)	A/B	Exports (A)	Imports (B)	A/B	Exports (A)	Imports (B)	A/B	Exports (A)	Imports (B)	A/B
1965	17	166	0.10	1,534	135	11.4	134	128	1.04	169	215	0.79	80	196	0.41
1967	27	239	0.11	1,747	166	10.5	172	161	1.07	196	231	0.85	95	223	0.43
1969	46	368	0.13	2,019	221	9.1	211	212	1.00	336	332	1.01	103	228	0.36
1971	60	488	0.12	2,546	241	10.6	288	270	1.07	398	467	0.85	157	426	0.37
1973	88	715	0.12	3,238	385	8.4	341	326	1.05	844	741	1.14	216	619	0.35
1975	161	712	0.23	—	—	—	—	—	—	—	—	—	308	834	0.37

Source: White Paper on Science and Technology, The Science and Technology Agency, Tokyo, 1976.
Note: The ratio of A/B for the years 1976, 1977 and 1978 in Japan are 0.20, 0.23 and 0.22 respectively.

countries, and how Japanese industries have grown on imported technology. For instance 96% of the techniques used by the synthetic fibre industry in Japan are improvements made to imported foreign technologies. The same figures with electronics, rubber products, electric machinery, automobile and chemical industries are respectively 82%, 80%, 72%, 65%, and 63%.[6] This improvement means that, although Japanese industries have been heavily dependent upon imported technologies, they have not only introduced and digested but also improved them.

The technical innovation (or improvement) has been found more in production processes than in products. It is ironical that Japan's defeat in the War helped to promote new processes. All major plants in Japan were destroyed, and industries could build optimally laid-out plants on the

TABLE 2.14 *Comparison of Research & Development*
expenditures

		R & D	
	Sales	sales	(%)
Chemical			
Du Pont	2,073,030	4.9	
American Cyanamid	533,961	3.3	
Mitsubishi Petrochemical	229,699	2.5	
Mitsui Petrochemical	150,138	2.8	
Machinery			
Caterpillar	1,224,630	3.5	
International Harvester	1,489,773	2.4	
Mitsubishi Heavy Industries	1,094,427	1.0	
Hitachi Shipbuilding	301,350	1.8	
Electric			
Western Electric	2,214,510	5.0	
General Electric	3,472,590	2.8	
Hitachi Ltd.	1,094,779	5.4	
Nippon Electric	385,826	4.3	
Automobile			
Ford	7,086,300	3.5	
Chrysler	2,263,321	3.2	
Toyota	1,473,852	1.5	
Honda	519,897	1.3	

Source: *The Weekly Diamond*, Tokyo, 4 October 1975.

vacant land. Various industries, with the help of the government, sent survey missions to the United States and tried to absorb as much advanced technology as possible. The lessons they brought back were: "the larger the plant, the lower the unit cost", and "the newer, the better".

These, so to speak, "basic" principles to be found in textbooks were promoted by the "theoretical" government officials along with the idea of "Scrap and Build". This meant that when a company presented application to the government to increase their production capacity by say 20%—as industries had to get their import quota for materials for building new plants and for energy resources for their operation, the company was "guided" to scrap the old capacity by say 5%. So the company made a 15% increase in their capacity, with much newer technology. Therefore, after the War, the Japanese steel industry has grown larger and larger by adopting newer and newer technology and building more and more efficient plants. In 1977, out of 15 of the largest blast furnaces in the world 10 were in Japan.

Most new and modern technology has been absorbed by Japanese industries, and a lack of Research & Development (R & D) capability could eventually undermine Japan's economic vigor.[7] Table 2.14 compares the R & D expenditures of Japanese and United States' companies. In spite of these gaps, however, Japanese industries seem to have begun to make "product innovation", too, as we find it now in quite a few products manufactured by Japanese companies.

Notes

1. *Mitsui Group: Perspective for the Future*, The Mainichi Newspapers, Tokyo, 1974.
2. See K. Bieda, *The Structure and Operation of the Japanese Economy*, John Wiley & Sons Australasia Pty. Ltd., 1970.
3. *Industrial Groupings in Japan*, Dodwell, Tokyo, 1975.
4. See M. Yoshino, *Japan's Managerial System*, The MIT Press, 1968, pp. 88 and 89.
5. Shigeto Tsuru, The End of the Miracle of Japanese Economy, *Ekonomisuto (Economist)*, The Mainichi Newspapers, May 1977.
6. K. Oshima, Setting the Scene Three: Japan, Chapter 4 in *Technological Innovation and the Economy*, Wiley-Interscience, 1970.
7. *Business Week*, 10 July, 1971, p. 42.

3

The Management of Human Resources

Japanese firms have quite different characteristics from those of the West. We saw in the last chapters something of the different ways in which they work and it may be that they are more authoritarian also. These factors alone cannot explain the effectiveness of Japanese management, however, and this chapter sets out to explore the organizational devices, in personnel and labour management, where the flow of human resources into, within and out of the firm plays a significant part. There are, in fact, two different streams—one of office workers or managers and the other of factory workers or labourers. Figure 3.1 illustrates the flow of human

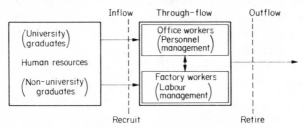

Fig. 3.1. Flow of human resources.

resources in three stages—inflow, throughflow and outflow. Each stage has features that are normal in Japan, but unusual in many other countries. The most characteristic of these is lifetime employment. One implication of this is that the "outflow" is normally into retirement. The first section of this chapter discusses the "inflow", mainly with reference to graduate recruits.

3.1 The Inflow

The manpower resources of a firm are university graduates and those who have completed their education at a high school or junior high. These two distinct sources of supply go into the offices and are handled by personnel managers, or onto the workshop floor where the control is through labour management. In this and the next sections we study chiefly university graduates. The recruitment of graduate workers normally takes place once a year at the time they complete their university courses. The employment system, which has up to now been dominant in Japanese firms, normally provides recruits with one chance in a lifetime to choose a firm. As will be demonstrated in the next chapter, the Japanese firm exists as a set of people rather than as a set of roles. This has a number of implications for the inflow of potential managers.

Firstly recruits do not choose a firm for the job or the monetary rewards but they choose a place to live in. In other words they decide which organization they will join without considering what job they will do. Likewise, the firm does not demand a specific man for a specific job. It wants a man who is adaptable. He should be, as the saying goes, as malleable as "mild steel". Figure 3.2 illustrates the difference from other systems. In the West, the relationships between p_i, a newly recruited member, and r_i, which is an individual role expected to be performed by p_i, is that of contract; in Japan the relationship is that of commitment. In the West the individual p_i is, in his lifetime, partially involved in the firm; but in Japan he is totally involved and is recruited by the firm to be one among an undifferentiated many. Accordingly the means and the content of the recruitment by firms in Japan places emphasis on the personality and

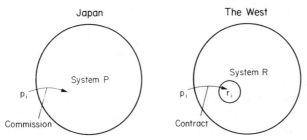

Fig. 3.2. Relationship between entrants and organization.

the character of the applicants in order that they should not damage the
climate of good human relations. In other words, to exaggerate slightly,
Japanese companies recruit school leavers without regard to what they
have studied. "The new recruits have been hired, not because of vocational
qualifications they already possess but because of personal and educational
characteristics."[1] This is closely related to the fact that in any organization
in Japan, due to historical and cultural reasons, job classification is vague;
as a result job requirements and qualifications are not clearly defined.[2]
Figure 3.3 shows how Japanese firms emphasize the result of interview
tests at recruitment, and what items are considered important. The sample
firms are the ones whose stocks are listed. These firms execute paper
tests on liberal arts, foreign languages, technical knowledges, and so forth.
But more than 75% of them make the interview more important than any
other consideration. At the end of the process, recruitment is not a
contractual event, but rather an irreversible decision where the applicants are being asked to commit themselves wholly to the firm, and
where the firm will guarantee employment for life. This necessitates
special care in the recruitment, and the following system has developed.

Character and personality	88.8%
Looks and attitudes	10.0%
Ability and knowledge	25.7%
Ambition and aggressiveness	77.1%
Career and family environment	9.5%
Others	1.3%

Fig. 3.3. Items evaluated to be important at the interview. *Source*:
Recruit '74, Japan Recruit Center, Tokyo, 1974.

The university year in Japan starts during April and ends in the following March. It is rare for a university graduate to gain employment at
any other time than April. Until the first of November of the previous
year, firms are barred from actually selecting recruits who are to start work
in the following April. Interviews, though not the actual selection, start at
the beginning of October. Students visit as many firms as possible during
that month. The ban on early recruitment is a gentlemen's agreement
advocated and strongly emphasized by Nikkeiren, the Japan Federation
of Employers' Association, which handles industrial relations. Although

this ban is at times secretly violated, the big firms usually obey it. The system creates a competition amongst the firms to secure the best students as soon as possible, and so firms have their own selection day after all on November 1st. Conversely this gives the students only one chance to apply to a big company.[3] For cultural and historical reasons applicants do not seek a specific job in the firm but apply to the firm itself. They are supposed to be as unmarked as a sheet of clean white paper. Graduates in the natural sciences are an exception, but even they are not so specialized as their counterparts in the West.

The process of application, selection and recruitment usually starts when a student reaches his fourth year. He starts applying to the firm he wishes to enter after the summer vacation. If he is of good quality and from a good university, he has a chance to get a tacit or tentative agreement to be employed by the firm before the deadline of November 1st. In most cases the firm asks a dozen or so universities to recommend a few students each year. Only those students recommended are allowed to take the entrance examination or interview on November 1st.

Fig. 3.4. Time schedule of recruitment.

3.2. The Throughflow

Management Development through Rotation

The uniqueness of the management development system in Japan lies rather in the on-the-job training by rotation than in outside education programmes. University leavers fit in well with this system. The day-to-day technical training or informal on-the-job training performed through the rotation period is considered to be a rational way of developing managers in a closed society like the Japanese.[4]

The most significant factor in rotation is the career programme. It has to be decided whether the company wants to develop specialists or generalists. Figure 3.5 illustrates the system.

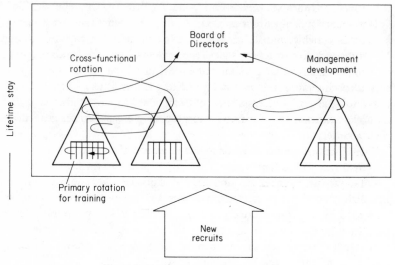

Fig. 3.5. Career programme on rotation.

At the lowest level a new recruit, say a university graduate of 22 or 23, enters a company. He is still a "layman", an undeveloped generalist who possesses only a broad background of education. After being assigned to a department with a particular function, he is regularly rotated from one section to another. While climbing up the seniority ladder this cross-sectional scales up to a cross-functional rotation and continues up to the age of around 40. During this process the manager is trained, mainly on the job, to be a specialist in each section and in each function. After his rotation finishes, he continues his development in one department while digesting his various experiences. By the time he reaches the top management level, he should be a generalist. Of course the smaller the area of the rotation, the more of specialist capacity he acquires. The length of stay at any given position is usually no longer than three years. The following example demonstrates the rotation of Mr. K. of Nippon Steel, a graduate of a university in metallurgy, up to 1972:

1954–1961, at a local plant:
  1954–7: as a foreman
  1957–60: in the quality control section

1960–1: as an open hearth section chief

1961–6, at the Tokyo head office:

1961–3: in Sohmu-Bu (a general affairs department) Duty: to study the possibility of technological cooperation with foreign companies in collaboration with a specialist in law.

1963–6: section chief in the Technology Development

1966–9, at a major plant:

1966–7: Director of a factory employing 600 workers in steel manufacture

1967–9: manager of the technology department

1969–72, at Tokyo head office:

1969–70: A member of the Organization Committee

1970–2: A manager in the Research and Development Department

1972 → Manager of the technology department, International Iron and Steel Institute.

Although it is open to question whether this process is normally undertaken as a thought-out long-term policy, it can be seen to produce high quality general managers. This kind of management training bears some resemblance, in its essence, to management education through action research. This technique has been described by its main exponent in the following terms:[5]

"On February 1, 1969, a party of twenty-one Belgian managers arrived in America; they had come to discuss, with professors at leading business schools and consultants from some of the world's largest corporations, a range of strategic problems encountered by their firms. To this extent, nothing was novel about their visit. In one way, however, it was probably unusual: each fellow had come to talk about the problem posed not by his own firm but by another also represented in the party."

"For several months, each of the visitors had worked full time in an enterprise other than his own, attacking a major managerial problem which he had not attacked before; in his pocket, he carried both a report of how he now saw the problem and a draft plan for dealing with it after he had returned to Europe . . ."

"Three weeks later, they were back in their Belgian foster enterprises, where they remained until the end of June, 1969" to make an "invasion of the boardroom by a senior manager from another enterprise".

This technique resembles the Japanese job rotation enlarged into a cross-company programme which develops managers both socially and individually. That is to say it develops management capacity externally to the firm, accumulating in each manager an individually developed resource. On the other hand the job rotation system in Japan develops management capacity internally with the firm and accumulates the developed resource as an organizational asset.

Job rotation between organizations is rare, but is exemplified in the career of Mr. F. of K. Bank:

1961–5 A local branch:
    1961–2 Deposit Department
    1962–4 Foreign Exchange Department
    1964–5 Investigation Department
1965 Tokyo Office, Personnel Department Training Section (Training at the Ministry of Finance)
1966 Ministry of Finance, Customs Bureau
1968 Back to K. Bank, Investigation Department
1971 Trainee at a Foreign Bank
1972 → K. Bank:
    1972–3 Foreign Department
    1973 → Planning Section

No scientific research has been done on the actual effect of job rotation on management development, but some possible hypotheses are discussed below. It has been supported by the affirmative responses of the audience and attendants of the author's speeches and seminars that the ability of a man to analyze is a decreasing function of age after above twenty-five and that the ability to synthesize is an increasing function up to possibly forty-five. Suppose that the former ability has to do with "specialization" and the latter produces "general management", which depends on a variety of experience, then the job rotation system meets two conflicting demands from the managerial point of view. The longer one stays in a post, the more specialized one becomes and opportunities for gaining a variety of experience are lost. Only well balanced and well-timed programmes can reconcile these conflicting demands. Although we do not yet have research data which might show whether the job rotation system of Japanese firms is more or less effective than other systems, we can at least affirm that the Japanese system is designed for allocating the limited time to the conflicting demands. In fact, the competence of Japanese middle managers to be decision orginators in the group decision-making system owes much to the job rotation system.

In addition to the formal effect of the rotation, what may be called the by-product consequences are important. As shown in Table 3.1, the employees' morale may be improved and with it human relations in the work place. Rotation gives wider human contacts in the firm to those rotated who will be promoted later. When they become middle managers, they need all the contacts they can get to generate the required consensus under the Ringi decision-making system (to be discussed in Chapter 4). The widened horizon gives them a widened set of living information from which may be derived decisions with a broader perspective. The following example of Mr. T. of the Dai-Ichi Kangyo Bank shows another feature of the system. A special characteristic in his case is the holding of a labour union post. A similar flow of managers between management and labour organizations is often seen in banks and insurance companies, but less often in manufacturing firms.

The Career Development of Mr. T. of DKB

1961–6 at a Branch: Cashier, deposit operator, book-keeper, loan section clerk, and customer section clerk.

1966–7 at an English conversation school.

1967–9 at Head Office—Foreign Exchange and Computer Section.

1969–70 at the Manchester Business School.

1970 (June to December) at the London Office:

    1971 at Head Office—Foreign Business Department.

   1971–3 in the International Department.

1973–4 on the Labour Union Executive Committee.

1974 → in a Branch, Foreign Exchange Department.

In Japanese companies most managers below section head join a union, and most firms have only one union. Therefore, the dichotomy between management and labour, which is found in the West, does not exist in the same form. As observed in other cases, university graduates are frequently placed and trained in factories and plants as ordinary workers for some time.

In these cases one by-product of the rotation is improved communication

TABLE 3.1 *Reasons for job rotation*

(%)

Number of employees	"The right person for the right job"	Education of the employees	Elevation of employees' morale	Satisfying employees' wish	Improvement of human relations	Expansion & reduction of particular departments
over 5,000	92.6	52.4	62.5	60.6	38.7	61.7
1,000–4,999	86.1	28.9	56.2	50.3	31.3	65.4
500–999	86.1	25.0	49.8	48.2	42.1	57.5
300–499	76.5	18.1	40.5	38.2	36.9	59.9
100–299	66.3	8.5	34.2	31.0	31.4	45.3
50–99	67.6	10.5	33.1	34.6	33.8	41.5
30–49	59.2	5.9	28.9	24.6	30.5	31.0

Source: Koyokanri no Jittai (The Actual State of Employment Management), Rodohorei Kyokai, Tokyo, 1974.
Note: The figures mean the ratio of firms which answered in the affirmative to the question.

between management and labour, and with it a better atmosphere on the shop floor. For example, during his stay at a local plant Mr. K. of Nippon Steel voluntarily taught workers metallurgy after working hours, and at a major plant he often had a party at his home and invited foremen and workers. One of the results of these close relationships was shown by the fact that the workers helped Mr. K. pack and send his belongings to Tokyo when he was moved to Head Office.

Formal Programme of Management Development

Table 3.2 shows the relative unimportance of investment in education and training in relation to other investments by Japanese firms in 1974 and 1975. No specific programmes of management training have been designed either in enterprises or in universities during the modernization of the Japanese economy. There has, indeed, been little communication between enterprises and universities. "Out of the total of 389 colleges and universities in Japan only 62, or 16%, have departments of business administration. Moreover, out of the total of 1,410,000 college students, only 100,000 (7%) are registered in these departments of business administration."[6] At present only one business school of a private

TABLE 3.2 *Classification of domestic investments*

Items	1974	1975
Production equipment	69.8	70.5
Land	6.0	4.7
Anti-pollution	9.3	10.6
R & D	1.8	1.6
Marketing	4.7	4.9
Education & training	0.2	0.1
Welfare	2.5	1.6
Others	5.7	6.0
Total	100.0	100.0

(%)

Source: *Japan Economic Journal*, Tokyo, 12 March, 1975.

MISJ - D

university, Keio, could be counted as an equivalent to those in the West.[7] This lack of formal training is reflected in the feeling among private companies that "the broad range of intellectual capability, decision-making ability and leadership . . . , were best developed through empirical means, while working".[8] Among various factors behind this the most important might be that in the process of their development Japanese companies have not had, at least up to very recent years, to develop their own management methods but to follow the systems developed in Europe before and in America after the War. Principles were to be found in text books always at hand whether they were applicable to their work or not. The system of lifetime employment results in the lack of intensive training programmes. A kind of lifetime training concept has been developed,[9] and the programmes are scattered extensively and thinly during the period of a man's stay in a company.

Lifetime employment and immobility in the labour market are, of course, two sides of a coin. These, along with the homogeneity of the Japanese people, have made corporate life resemble a *Gemeinschaft* community. This kind of climate and situation in the company is supposed to have made the community-member unrecognized as a possessor of man-power. He is, in other words, not treated as one of the resources of production. So programmes for increasing the productivity of the "re-source", his training, are also apt to be unrecognized. Finally the fact that wages and salaries in Japan are dependent almost solely on seniority does not generate in the individual an incentive for training himself. If he develops his capacity, he cannot get a higher wage or salary.

The phenomenon of the entrant disappearing into the organization to become an anonymous element of manpower can be expected to bring about a unique process in management development and training. The training is of at least two types, one of which is for new entrants under-taken in the first year and lasting from a few days to a whole year; the other is for developing middle management. Table 3.3 is an example of the training programme performed by Toyo Rayon for new entrants. Group Guidance and the Group Discussion are meant to cultivate "the attitude of mind of an organization man". And the morning run is expected to "train physical strength to endure the corporate life".

Evidence of the process of becoming an anonymous element in the organization can be found in a training programme produced by Toyota

Motors: This consists of on-the-job training, off-the-job programmed education and human relations activities. The off-the-job programme for university graduates lasts for the first 11 months, and carries every attribute of the training philosophy of the company as Table 3.4 shows. In this table sales practice and work practice especially demonstrate the characteristics of the anonymous element, and along with these two practices that of office business is a condensed form of the whole manpower development by rotation system which is commonly to be seen up to middle management level in Japanese firms. The object of these training programmes is to stimulate creativity, to promote an aggressive spirit and to promote the spirit of the organization man.

The system of rotation, based on lifetime employment, is designed to transform "the vocationally-untrained recruits from the schools into an efficient occupationally-structured work force".[10] Naturally the system is not sufficient by itself and needs to be supplemented by formal training programmes. As shown in Fig. 3.6, during the 12 months which ended in

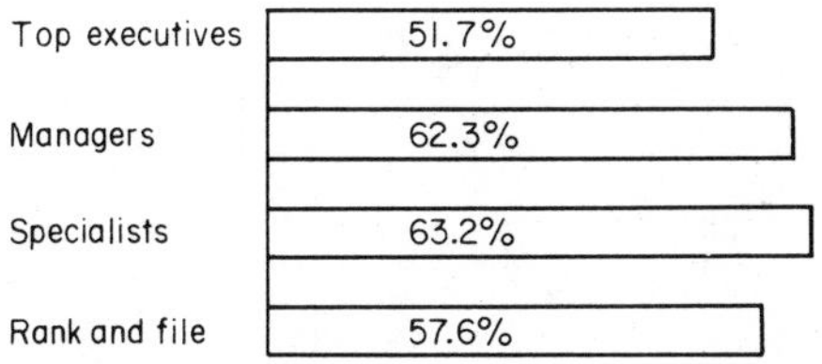

Top executives   51.7%

Managers   62.3%

Specialists   63.2%

Rank and file   57.6%

Fig. 3.6. Ratio of businessmen who received management education between September 1972 and August 1973. *Source*: *Kigyo-jin-kyoiku no Kihonteki Vision* (*Fundamental Vision of Management Education*), Institute of Business Administration and Management, Tokyo, 1974.

August 1973 more than half of Japanese businessmen passed through some education programme. For Japanese firms, however, the major training programmes are internal. Because of the emphasis placed on informal and on-the-job training, off-the-job programmes are usually short-term as is shown in Fig. 3.7. The contents of these programmes are not very different from those in the West. Most characteristic of Japanese firms is the training programme for new recruits which seems to have condensed the essence of the long-term career programme. It is usual during the training

TABLE 3.3 *The Orientation programme for new personnel (new university graduates) The First Half*

Hour / Date	9:00	10:00	11:00	12:00	13:00	14:00	15:00	16:00	17:00	18:00	19:00
April 1	Orientation		Entrance Ceremony	Luncheon Party	Speech by the President		Introduction of the Entrants			Group Guidance 1	
2		Group Discussion (1)			Report of the Discussion		Speech by Mr. Nakayama "Creative Thinking"	Group Guidance 2			
3		"Basic Philosophy of Personnel Management" E.V.P. of P.M. Dept.			Recreation	Group Discussion (2)	Group Discussion (2)			Friendship Party	
4		"Domestic Sales"	"Export Activity"		Explanation of the Business (Textile Sales)		"Desirable Figure for Sales Activity"				
5		Study Trip to Shiga Plant									
6 (Sun.)											
7	"Production Activity"		"Overseas Business"		Explanation of the Business (Textile Production)			"Materials Supply Condition"			
8	Study Trip to Film Mill and Laboratory				Speech by the Vice President			"The Present and the Future of the Plastic Dept."			
9	Trip to Engineering Laboratory	"Engineering of Our Company"			Explanation of the Business (Plant Construction)			"Industrial Relations Management"			

Day						
10	"Planning Activity"	Study Trip to Seta Plant				
11	Study at the Textile Laboratory	Study and Explanation at R & D Laboratory				
12	"EDP System and the Use of Computers"	Speech by Mr. Kikukawa, Managing Director			"Personnel Mgt."	
13 (Sun.)						Personal Interview (1)
14	"Profit Control"	"Labour Union"	Recreation	Speech by the Vice President	Speech by the Chairman	Personal Interview (2)
15	"R & D Activity"	"Toray Industrial Group"	Movies on the business	"How to Produce the Work"		Personal Interview (3)
16	Anniversary Ceremony of the Company					

Source: 70 *nendai no Shimnyu Shain Kyoiku* (Introductory Education for New University Graduates in the Seventies), Nikkeiren, Tokyo, 1970.

TABLE 3.4 *Training programme for the new recruits of the Toyota Motor Co.*

Sept. (1968)– March (1969)	Communication before the entrance	Mailing "History of Toyota", pamphlets of Toyota's products, the company newspaper, and opinions of seniors to the would-be entrants for pre-education.
April (1969)	Introductory education	Speeches by directors, explanation of the company rules, necessary procedures, and trips to factories.
	Work practice	Work with workers in just the same way on the shop floor of the production process.
May (1969)	Office business practice	Experience business at the production control department, the engineering department, the accounting department, etc.
	Survey on production process	Survey and report on the production process of a part from its input to completion.
June (1969)	Practice of automobile structure	Taking to pieces and assembling a car.
	Preliminary education of sales practice	
July–Sept. (1969)	Sales practice	All trainees with any background and education work at dealers' shops as a mere salesman who should do every sales activity.
Oct. (1969)	Work practice	Another work practice as a finish of this introductory and orienting education.
Nov. (1969)– Feb. (1970)	Preliminary placement practice	Deciding to place whom to what job, and then each trainee practices the job and writes a report on a given theme about it.
March (1970)	Formal placement	

Source: *70 nendai no Shinnyu Shain Kyoiku* (Introductory Education for New University Graduates in Seventies), Nikkeiren, Tokyo, 1970.

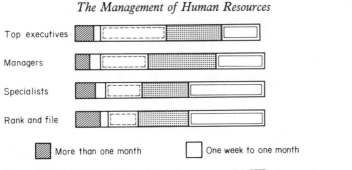

Fig. 3.7. Term of on-the-job training. *Source*: The same as Fig. 3.6.

period for the new recruits to lodge together and sometimes even have a marathon session in the early morning for "spiritual training". They may also practice *Zen* at temples or, in some firms, experience a few days disciplined life at military bases.

A survey published by the Ministry of Labour in 1972 showed that about 80% of companies in the sample were not satisfied with their in-company training programmes. Among the reasons for this were the short time allowed as a result of the scarcity of manpower, the difficulty in securing good lectures and instructors, the lack of suitable equipment and facilities and poorly organized systems for the training. Some of the results are shown in Table 3.5.

As for training outside the company, there are few independent institutions of management education available. University business schools do not have courses for businessmen, except for the one at Keio, and among the independents only the Institute for International Studies and Training runs a course for as long as a year on a full-time basis. This institute was established by a Government measure in 1967 to develop management resources for international business operations. Other institutions, including the Japan Productivity Centre, have various programmes but only on a part-time basis. Clearly if Japanese companies wish to send their managers for training outside organization, there are not many available. This may well have increased the tendency for many firms, especially large ones, to build their own training centres and thus reduce still further the demand for outside institutions.

TABLE 3.5 *Ratio of employees dissatisfied with the company training programmes*

	Technical specialists, researchers & managers (%)	Office workers (%)	Foremen & supervisors (%)	Skilled workers (%)	Ordinary workers (%)	Others (%)
Satisfied	22.8	18.7	42.4	27.7	26.0	23.3
Dissatisfied	48.8	40.3	32.5	40.3	33.6	28.8
Neither	24.9	33.2	19.7	25.2	34.9	32.9
No answer	3.5	7.9	5.3	6.9	5.5	15.1
Reasons for the dissatisfaction						
Training only for the present job	15.7	19.6	19.2	35.2	38.8	38.1
No systematic training	61.4	54.7	51.5	36.3	37.5	47.6
To attend after working hours & on holidays	9.0	4.1	7.1	10.4	7.9	14.3
Limited number of trainees	7.1	7.4	10.1	12.6	11.3	—
Limited class of trainees	17.6	25.7	21.2	30.8	25.4	19.0
Others	16.7	8.8	13.1	6.0	13.8	28.6

Source: Rodosha-no Kyoiku-kunren-ni Kansuru Ishiki Chosa (A Research on Consciousness of Employees concerning Education and Training), Ministry of Labour, 1972.

The Social Implications of Management Development

Where there is mobility across firms there is a social mechanism for levelling differences of productivity and the value of the human resources. This mechanism could be expected to give society an "optimal" allocation of resources. But in Japan, where nearly 60% of the executives of 300 large companies stay for life in the same firm, the allocation of manpower is, of course, restricted within the company. The difference between these two mechanisms is that in the former the allocation in general is left to an invisible hand, but in the latter to a planning hand.

The planning hand comes into effect, as already demonstrated, principally through the rotation system within the company. But the lack of manpower mobility, catalyzed by the climate of a Gemeinschaft-type community, reduces the likelihood of the company considering manpower as a resource. This, of course, fits in well with the Japanese wage and salary system which is based almost entirely on seniority. All these factors have resulted in a lack of objective measures to evaluate individual capacity. As a result both companies and employees seem to be less eager for individual than for organizational development. This tendency is illustrated in Table 3.6. Thus the system of management development and training in Japan is geared to producing general managers rather than functional specialists. If it were possible to compare the capacity for individual action, it can be assumed that western managers would rate more highly than Japanese; but when it comes to effectiveness within an organization, the position is reversed. This is strongly to the advantage of the Japanese, because the effectiveness of the organization is not the mere sum of individual actions. On the other hand, the capability of the Japanese manager is reduced when he is severed from his organization. His relationship to his firm has been described as chemical rather than physical.

The Japanese system, which might be called confined management development, has its merits. Firstly it is almost perfectly controlled within the company because of the lack of mobility, and secondly it can be planned on a long-term basis because of the lifetime employment. These are obvious reasons for preferring in-company training. Table 3.7 demonstrates the situation. Each company has its own climate, and those who enter, stay and develop there are trained for that special climate, and in most cases lose their availability to other companies. This causes the problem that

TABLE 3.6 *Pattern of training desired*

Class / Pattern	Top executives (%)	Managers (%)	Specialists (%)	Rank and file (%)
On-the-job training	19.9	23.9	20.1	25.8
Job rotation	11.7	12.1	12.7	11.8
Off-the-job training by the class	21.5	31.3	12.4	9.5
Off-the-job training by the function	3.3	3.7	16.9	13.6
A workshop all at once	7.4	7.7	9.5	21.5
Support for self development	36.2	21.3	28.4	17.8

Source: *Kigyo-jin-kyoiku no Kihonteki Vision* (Fundamental Vision of Management Education), Institute of Business Administration and Management, Tokyo, 1974.

those developed and trained management resources are held exclusively in each company to become a monopolized asset.

3.3 Aspects of Labour Management Relevant to Corporate Decision-making

Before World War II, Japanese products had a reputation for low prices, low quality and production by cheap labour. But, as a result of the rapid growth of the economy after the War, labour has become as expensive as in the United States and Europe; and the products are no longer either low price or low quality. They may not be highly innovative, but they are not copies and are overwhelmingly competitive in quality in the world markets. The quality improvement is mainly due to the innovations in the production process described elsewhere which have centred on the introduction of rigorous quality control. And the quality control has been

TABLE 3.7 *Pattern of training*

(Multiple answer)

Number of Employees	5,000 or over (%)	1,000–4,999 (%)	500–999 (%)	300–499 (%)	100–299 (%)	50–99 (%)	30–49 (%)
At the facility within the firm	98.9	98.8	96.6	94.7	84.0	71.4	60.2
At other firms in Japan	28.2	26.8	24.2	22.6	22.0	25.6	17.5
At universities or training schools	35.0	18.9	9.3	9.0	7.2	8.3	2.5
Jointly with other firms	18.9	15.9	24.9	25.1	31.8	34.7	30.8
At foreign firms	28.9	11.6	6.5	3.5	2.6	—	0.1
At foreign universities or training schools	24.9	9.0	2.5	2.1	0.2	2.2	—
Others	15.9	21.4	22.5	25.1	12.5	19.2	16.1

Source: Koyokanri no Jittai (The Actual State of Employment Management), Rodohorei Kyokai, Tokyo, 1974.

supported and promoted by various movements on the shop floor such as QC Circle or Zero Defects.[12]

These activities would be impossible without company-wide physical and mental support, which is partly provided by the labour union. Usually a firm has a union which consists of both factory and clerical workers up to the section chief level, and this union belongs to a federation for the particular industry. For example, the Nippon Steel Labour Union is a member of the Japanese Federation of Iron and Steel Industry Workers' Unions.

A federation of unions usually joins one of a few central organizations. Table 3.8 shows the degree of unionization by size of establishment.

TABLE 3.8 *Estimated rate of union organization in the private sector by size of establishment*

(%)

Size of establishment	All industries	Manufacturing
All establishments	28.0	37.9
500 or more employees	63.6	76.0
100–499 employees	31.5	37.2
30–99 employees	9.0	10.1
29 or less employees	3.4	1.3

Source: *Basic Survey of Trade Unions*, Ministry of Labour, 1974.

Although the initiative for wage negotiations is taken by the central organization at the same time each spring, which is therefore called the "Spring Offensive", the details of the agreement are worked out in each firm. The firms, themselves, exchange information about a possible new level of wages. Table 3.9 shows that among foreign affiliated companies in Japan the higher the ratio of the Japanese share, the more they exchange information on wages with other Japanese firms. This is one way in which Japanese firms try to keep in step with one another. The Spring Offensive is a kind of wage equalization mechanism in a situation lacking labour mobility. It brings about the same kind of bargaining power as that of trade unions, but company unions naturally let each worker be interested in the profitability of the company.

TABLE 3.9 *Concerning wages do you exchange
information with: (foreign affiliated companies)*

(%)

Ownership share	Foreign affiliated companies	Japanese companies	None
Less than 45	6.7	64.0	29.3
45–50	9.3	50.7	41.4
50–95	18.6	25.6	58.1
Over 95	30.3	22.8	53.8
Foreign companies	88.3	21.7	10.0

Source: *A Survey on Industrial Relations of Foreign Affiliated Companies in Japan*, Ministry of Labour, 1978.

In parallel with this there is lifetime employment or, more exactly, a much lower labour turnover than in the West. It is often said that lifetime employment was established, combined with the fixing of wages and salaries by length of service, by capitalism to secure skilled labour forces and good managers when they were scarce, especially after the War. Here we do not go into the history of the employment system but take it as it is and examine the effect. The system, which severely restricts the mobility of labourers and also managers, is deeply ingrained in the Japanese consciousness. The support of long established sentiments, like the "familyism" already described, have made it a moral issue together with the wage system which derives from it. The effects of this system are shown in Table 3.10, where they can clearly be seen to restrict mobility even further. Thus a worker moving from one company to another in 1973, aged between 30 and 34, could only expect to receive 75% of the wage of a similar worker in his new company who had worked there since leaving school. But here we should not make the hasty conclusion that the workers in Japan are miserably treated. It is really difficult to tell which is the hen and which is egg. Namely it is not certain whether the sentiment among workers which rejects "job hopping" created the wage system or the system created not only physical but mental immobility. Perhaps it is both.

TABLE 3.10 *The first wage of the*
"non-standard" worker

(%)

Age classes	The ratio of the first wage to the wage of "Standard" worker			
	1967	1970	1972	1973
25–29	81	83	81	81
30–34	74	76	73	75
35–39	67	71	70	71
40–49	56	60	59	59
50–59	52	56	54	55

Standard worker: A worker who enters a firm immediately after graduating a school and continues working in the firm.

Non-standard worker: A worker who enters a firm not immediately after graduating a school and has not worked over a year in the firm.

Source: *Wage Census*, Rodo Horei Kyokai, Tokyo, 1973.

In spite of the stability of the labour force, Japanese managers are still reluctant to introduce participation as increasingly practiced in Europe. According to a report by the Tokyo Chamber of Commerce, 83.3% of managers are against formal labour participation on the board. Most of them (84.6%) judge that only a joint council is desirable. Another group of managers, Keizai Doyu Kai, presented a report on this problem in May 1976. They suggested that the style of decision-making in Japanese firms, carries with it inherent participation and that in current labour practices there already exist various alternative mechanisms to labour participation.

Table 3.11 shows the present status of the management-labour council in domestic and in foreign-affiliated firms. The table demonstrates that the large Japanese firm is more likely to have a council. A fact that emerges on foreign affiliated firms in Japan is that the smaller the foreign share, the larger is the proportion having a council. Table 3.12 shows that the smaller the foreign ownership, or the larger the Japanese share, the more sympathetic are the attitudes of management towards the unions. Among the foreign affiliated firms having a management-labour council, as Table 3.13 shows, the larger the foreign share, the smaller is the proportion of firms whose management-labour council discusses such corporate or administrative items as investment plans or personnel problems.

TABLE 3.11 *"Do you have a regular management-labour council?"*

Japanese companies		Foreign affiliated companies	
Employees number	Yes (%)	Ownership share (%)	Yes (%)
10,000 and over	98.1	less than 45	58.7
5,000–9,999	93.3	45–50	53.3
1,000–4,999	94.0	50–95	18.6
500–999	84.8	over 95	30.3
300–499	80.0	Foreign companies	20.0
299 and less	69.2		

Sources: *A Survey on the Present Status of Management-Labour Council in Japan*, Japan Productivity Center, Tokyo, 1976. *A Survey on Industrial Relations of the Foreign Affiliated Companies in Japan*, Ministry of Labour, 1978.

Note: Of foreign affiliated companies, 54.9% are American.

TABLE 3.12 *Attitudes of foreign affiliated companies toward labour unions*

Ownership share (%)	Admit full-time officers	Provide unions with office room
less than 45	51.0	88.2
45–50	49.2	84.2
50–95	25.0	83.3
over 95	9.8	53.7
foreign companies	8.7	47.8

Source: *A Survey on Industrial Relations of Foreign Affiliated Companies in Japan*, Ministry of Labour, 1978.

TABLE 3.13 *Items discussed by management-labour council (foreign affiliated companies)*

Ownership share (%)	Investment plan and administrative	Personnel management
less than 45	77.3	68.2
45–50	71.1	65.3
50–95	62.5	75.0
over 95	38.6	52.3
foreign companies	16.7	33.3

Source: *A Survey on Industrial Relations of Foreign Affiliated Companies in Japan*, Ministry of Labour, 1978.

TABLE 3.14 *Do you think officers of labour unions have technical knowledge for discussing management?*

A. *Companies*

Size	10,000 and over	5,000–9,999	1,000–4,999	500–999	300–499	less than 300 (%)
Yes	57.7	42.9	25.0	14.3	—	35.7
Not sufficient	26.9	39.3	54.4	71.4	82.4	42.9
Can't tell which	15.4	17.8	20.6	14.3	17.6	21.4

B. *Labour Unions*

Size	10,000 and over	5,000–9,999	1,000–4,999	500–999	300–499	less than 300 (%)
Yes	21.7	12.0	18.6	13.8	14.3	6.7
Not sufficient	65.2	84.0	95.2	75.9	85.7	86.6
Can't tell which	13.1	4.0	6.2	10.3	—	6.7

Source: A Survey on the Present Status of Management – Labour Council in Japan, Japan Productivity Center, Tokyo, 1976.

A very interesting fact is demonstrated by Table 3.14. It is that management has a higher opinion of the ability of the union officials to discuss administrative affairs than the officials themselves.

It may be said that familyism between management and labour exists in Japanese firms, but consensus formation has been limited so far within certain plants and factories. It is also often true that some problems that are vital to the survival of a firm, such as a merger with another or an appointment of a new president, have to be the subject of an agreement in advance with senior union officials. A merger, which is a marriage of two "families", is impossible without union agreement in each family.

Notes

1. *Manpower Policy in Japan*, OECD, Paris, 1973, p. 138.
2. See Allen Dickerman, *Training Japanese Managers*, Praeger, 1974.
3. Allen Dickerman, *ibid.*, pp. 24 and 25.
4. T. Ono, Jinteki Nohryoku no Kaihatsu to Katsuyo (Development and Utilization of Manpower), a chapter in *Keiei Jinji*, Diamond Publishing Co., Tokyo, 1971.
5. See Reginald W. Revans, *Developing Effective Managers*, Preager, 1971. (The quoted sentences are quoted with the permission of the author.)
6. I. Ueno, The Situation of Management Education in Japan, in *Management Education*, OECD, Paris, 1972, pp. 38 and 39.
7. In Japan, contrary to the West, the world of education and intellectuals has been dominated by a few governmental universities with Tokyo University at the top.
8. I. Ueno, *op. cit.*, p. 37.
9. See P. F. Drucker, What we can learn from Japanese Management, *Harvard Business Review*, March–April 1971.
10. *Manpower Policy in Japan*, OECD, Paris, 1973, p. 138.
11. As for this, see Time Market Research Report, No. 1796, *Asia: The Man in Charge*, Time Inc., 1973.
12. As for QC Circle, see N. Sasaki and D. Hutchins (ed.), *The Japanese Approach to Product Quality Management*, Pergamon, 1981 (to be published).

4

The Decision-making
Mechanism

The traditional way of organizational decision-making in Japan is the Ringi system, which crystallizes every characteristic of the mechanism. First, we shall see what it is, and then try to get deeper insights into it.

4.1 The Ringi System

The Ringi system of organizational decision-making in the Japanese organization was used before the industrialization and modernization started in the middle of the 19th century. It is believed that the feudal political order in Japan gave birth to this system where the substantial job of policy-making was left to the lower-upper or upper-middle level members of the hierarchy in order to make it possible for the top to escape from taking the responsibility by imputing it to those who made the drafts of the policies. The top leaders in the power structure holding the actual authority were thereby left untouched. The Ringi system was then nothing but a product of the totalitarian feudalism in the Tokugawa Era which lasted for more than two centuries before the Meiji Restoration. When Japan started her modernization and industrialization in the Meiji Era, the Ringi system was smoothly brought into the new bureaucracy of the Meiji Government. In parallel with this those public corporations and private companies established under the leadership of the Government combined this system with the modern management system introduced from the West. What is important to note is that the introduction of the rational system from the West preceded the establishment of individualism which should be brought forth by way of spiritual revolution. The birth of individualism, even if being incomplete, had to wait for the end of World War II.

The word *ringi* means obtaining approval on a proposed matter through the vertical, and sometimes horizontal, circulation of documents to the concerned members in the organization. As an administrative procedure it consists of four steps; proposal, circulation, approval and record. The typical procedure is such as described below.[1]

In a section of a department a middle management presents a good idea for a new sales campaign. The *Kacho*, the section chief, therefore calls a meeting of his section. Through discussion to boil down the factors of the idea they judge that they will need the overall support of the firm. The *Kacho* reports this to his *Bucho*, the department head, and consults with him. The *Bucho* also agrees that it is a good idea. It is at this point that the time-consuming activity of getting a general consensus starts. Up to this point a local consensus in this section has been reached. Next, a wider agreement in the department is sought. Then an overall consensus in the firm is tried to be attained, possibly through meetings with other departments concerned arranged by the *Bucho*, as an information exchange process. Each department sends one *Bucho*, one *Kacho* and perhaps two *Kakaricho*, sub-section chiefs. If there are four departments involved, in all 16 to 20 members will attend the meeting. If they need the opinion of specialists on the shop floor, they will invite engineers or sometimes foremen to their meetings. The initiator and his consonant colleagues, under the leadership of the *Kacho*, run about formally and informally from section to section and from department to department to prepare the necessary documents and materials. This prior coordination is vital for the Ringi system to be effective.

It is only after the moment when the department judges to have attained an informal agreement from all of the other departments concerned that the formal procedure starts. This is the circulation of a formal document of request, the *Ringi-sho* (paper or document), for approval or authorization of the proposal. All of the responsible managers concerned affix their seals to it as a sign of agreement. (In Japan seals are used for signing instead of a signature.) The number of seals can reach ten or twelve. In order for this circulation to be carried out the details of the plan are completed by the members of the original section. The *Ringi-sho* finally goes up to the top decision-making body for formal authorization and the final "go-ahead".

This is a somewhat simplified example of the Ringi system. There are other cases where the initiator is the head of a department or the *Kacho* of a section or an even higher echelon manager. But in most cases the initiator belongs to the middle management. Even if the initiator is a *Bucho* or a *Kacho*, however, in almost every case he will give his idea to his subordinate(s) and let him (them) propose it. What is important is that, unlike the feudal system, the responsibility is rarely imputed to the middle management. It keeps lying in the hands of the seniors.

After the War, as described later again, because of the purge of the older managers (over 40 or 50), younger members of the middle management had to take the responsibility of running the company. One after another they were sent to the United States to bring back the American way of management. As a result it became almost fashionable to "purge" the "feudal" system for the following reasons: the lack of leadership at the top; the inflexibility or narrowness of the drafts drawn by the middle management compared with those of the top management; the vagueness of the boundaries of authority and responsibility; the prior coordination, which takes into account as many comments, advice and opinions as possible from other departments concerned, may often make the final plan a product of compromise; the formality of the system is apt to be inefficient; the excess of *Ringi-sho* for the top management to check makes them only a stamping machine. Accordingly it is often said that the traditional Ringi system is now disappearing. Perhaps the use of the *Ringi-sho* is decreasing, but it is unlikely that the underlying spirit of the system is dying. It may be time-consuming and politically delicate but it is very appropriate for the Japanese organization based on and protected by seniority. Here, like the feudal system, it is the middle management who take or are expected to take the initiative in making proposals and in making the substantial decisions, and the seniors manage the political affairs and arrangements to back them up. "To manage a seniority organization efficiently really needs a senior man."[2] Under lifetime employment the seniors have stayed in a firm longer than the middle management, therefore, they know better what's what and who's who in their firm. Japanese organizations, where personal affairs and human relations should be paid due consideration, are not the place for the 1% of geniuses but for the 99% of ordinary people. Individual conspicuousness might destroy the harmony within the organization.

Ironically it was by Americans that the merits of the Ringi system were found. They were, for instance, J. C. Abbegglen, Peter Drucker and other managers who stayed some years in Japan on business. The biggest merit found was participation, in the Japanese way. Under the Ringi system many people including lower management automatically participate in the decision-making process. In addition to this, "there are four primary advantages: fewer aspects of the decision are overlooked; the trauma that accompanies change is reduced; participants feel committed to implementing a decision they have helped to formulate; and far bolder decisions can be made".[3]

When we measure the efficiency of management not only from the time needed for the decision but also from the time needed for implementation, the whole process, namely the former plus the latter, may be shorter for Japanese firms than for Western. This is due to the fact that in Japanese firms, after the thorough and overall discussion before decisions are made and after the consensus has been reached, no objection occurs in the implementation process.[4]

There is no denying that the rapid growth of the Japanese economy after the War was supported by this organizational decision-making system. Deeper insights and analyses may be needed to find the managerial reasons for the growth. The following sections are an effort towards that objective.

4.2 The Application of Systems Concept

The firm is a set of people, and at the same time it is a set of roles to be performed by this set of people. Each of the two sets is "an organized or complex whole".[5] For convenience let us call the set of people System P, and the set of roles System R. The components of the two systems will be called p_i and r_i respectively, where r_i is a role expected to be performed by p_i. Then System P may be represented by $\sum p_i$, namely a certain number of people brought together to form an organization. In the case of System R, it is assumed that a firm has its role as the whole of R. It is then partitioned into component parts each of which is a role or a task that is expected to be

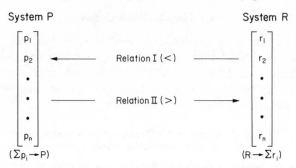

Fig. 4.1. Human system and role system.

performed by each member of System P. From this it follows that System R is a set of individual roles to be represented as $\sum r_i$. There are two systems of relations between System P and System R, ignoring any possible gap between the coverage of the two systems. Figure 4.1 describes the relationships.

In Relationship I, System R dominates System P, as is indicated by the direction of the inequality sign in parentheses. Here the role of the firm is partitioned into individual roles for the individual member of System P ($R \to \sum r_i$), and each individual role r_i demands a person p_i who is expected to perform the role. The acceptance of r_i by p_i is a contract.

In Relationship II System P dominates System R. A set of people is formed ($\sum p_i \to P$) which then explores what it can or should do. Although the result is the same in that p_i performs r_i, the boundary of the individual roles is vague. This relationship can be described as *gemeinschaftlich*.

In the West, Relationship I is prevalent, and in Japan, Relationship II. If the existing principles and concepts of organizational behaviour, that have been developed in the West relating to the decision-making process, are re-examined in contrasting Relationship I with Relationship II, light is shed on the decision-making mechanisms of Japanese firms which otherwise appear incomprehensible to the Westerner. Relationships I and II demand different value systems for their base. Therefore, in order to understand Relationship II a drastic inversion of Western value criteria is necessary.

4.3 The Decision Codes

Table 4.1 shows an international comparison of Japanese decision-making style with that of other Asians. Though not fully revealed in these figures, here we find explicitly and implicitly such often cited characteristics of the Japanese decision-making codes as harmony, consensus, seniority, paternalism, collectivism, and so on.

TABLE 4.1 *Comparison of Japanese decision-making style with that of other Asians*

(Q) How are important purchasing decisions usually made in your company? (Please check only one.)

(A)

	Japan (%)	S.E. Asia (%)
One man decides	3	5
One man decides based on recommendations of technical personnel	22	52
Several individuals must approve	32	27
Group consensus	38	13
No response	5	3
	100%	100%
Number of responses	356	894

(Quoted, with permission, from *Asia: The Men in Charge*, Time Market Research Report No. 1796, 1973.)

Paternalism and harmony are pervasive decision codes in any organization in the Japanese society. The extreme case is found in the following statement by Mr. Ishida, a past president of Idemitsu Petroleum Company.

"The Philosophy of Idemitsu is, to put it briefly, application of Japanese home life to enterprise. Since the first day of our business we have endeavoured to bring our employees up men of good character, because they were left to us by their parents.

In response to that expectation we thought it the first necessity to give them a place to live in. So even during the very poor years after World

War II we put the first priority on the construction of dormitories and company-houses for them. Our company is our home. We do not have, therefore, any time-card system. We do not have any definite age for retirement. Our basic principle is to respect harmonious personal relations."[6]

The dizziest sight to Westerners may be the company song often sung in Japanese firms. The following example is that of the Matsushita Electric Industrial Co.:

"For the building of a new Japan
Let's put our strength and minds together
Doing our best to promote production,
Sending our goods to the people of the world,
Endlessly and continuously,
Like water gushing from a fountain.
Grow, industry, grow, grow, grow
Harmony and Sincerity
Matsushita Electric."[7]

However, if we consider the Japanese firms to be a set of people or a community such as a fraternity club or alumni association, it might be less extraordinary to see the workers sing their company songs. The same kind of spirit is to be found in articles of association or incorporation. Although often being abstract, they are an expression of organizational decision codes. A few typical ones are shown below.[8]

Sumitomo Metal
Firstly pay consideration to tradition, the nation and the society. Set much value on getting trust from others and giving them assurance. Work together in an organization. Respect people and technology.

Kubota Industrial Machinery
Kubota is a company to respect the nation.
Kubota is a company to respect the user.
Kubota is a company not forgetting *On*.*
Be a company of humanity.
On is favour which was given in the past.

Takeda Chemical
Set value on harmony.

What is important here is to duly consider the basic differences between Relation I and Relation II described earlier. In the West the firm is over-whelmingly an economic entity. In Japan it is primarily a social entity though operating in an economic environment. Management principles developed in the West may be those which can be applied on the first day to set up a firm. But as a matter of fact, 99% or more of the existing firms are literally going concerns. Namely, only such principles of management as those which take it to be a premise that the present members of the organization will stay for the remainder of their careers are applicable. This posture may indeed seem too exaggerated but where the *raison d'être* of the firm is different, different principles of management must be applied.

For instance, in the following analysis by Miller and Simonetti, socio-cultural variables and management practices of Japan and Great Britain seem to be almost identical (without considering whether the original analyses by Harbison and Scott are correct).[9]

However, the output (i.e., management effectiveness) is completely different in the two countries, which may be a result of the basic differences between Relationship I and II. So far quite a bit of research has been done on the socio-cultural factors and their functions within the Japanese firm. In looking at these factors alone, however, as shown in this analysis, a proper explanation of the Japanese management system is almost impossible.

In this book, we are not going deeper in an analysis of socio-cultural factors. They are to be considered decision (value) premises given from outside of the decision-making process. Although a minimum necessity in the organizational context to dissolve them into endogenous variables will be retained as follows, they are treated as exogenous variables in our scheme.

Management in Japan, especially after World War II, has been management for growth. Growth cannot be produced by stagnant management. It must be a product of dynamic and innovative management. This means that the behaviour of Japanese firms has been dynamic and innovative. Actually, their decision shown in the pursuit of "scale merit" and in the strategies for growth have been very bold. Then, the codes of the decisions or the value systems of the firms must have been also bold and innovative.

Since the end of the war, there has been an almost complete separation of ownership and management in Japan. From the standpoint of "the

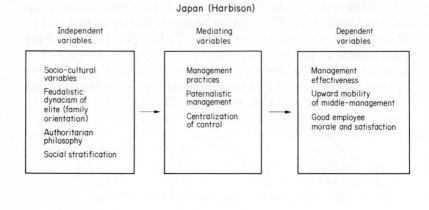

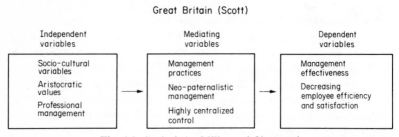

Fig. 4.2. Analysis by Miller and Simonetti.

theory of the firm", this may be a major factor in the growth of Japanese firms.[10] Professional managers are to pursue the growth of the firm rather than profit.

Though some organizational and managerial factors have been introduced, there is still not much difference in theory between the motive of the managers and that of the firms. That is, there is not any heterogeneity between the two. A "mob psychology" effect should be considered.

As we already know from Chapter 1, the individual decision codes of the Japanese could not be described as "dynamic, innovative and bold". It might also be true that individual "followership" has led to company "followership" and that this behaviour is evident in the chain reaction of collective investment in equipment by Japanese firms.

Generally speaking, Japanese firms do not have individual leadership but group leadership. What is very important here is how individual "followership" is transformed into group leadership and through what organizational process individual passiveness is changed into collective activeness. We can not induce a dynamic and innovative set of organizational decision codes from a simple aggregation of non-innovative and reserved sets of individual decision codes.

Fig. 4.3. Transformation of decision codes.

Then, as the above figure shows, some type of quality transformation process is necessary to change the passive decision codes of the individual members into the active codes of the firm. An organizational device is necessary for this transformation.

To return to our analysis, the component of System P, p_i, is the smallest decision-making unit in the organization of the firm. Decisions by the smallest units add up to make a group decision, and those by groups make up an organizational decision. Likewise the codes of the smallest unit are integrated into the group codes, and the latter are integrated into the firm's codes. It is the codes of the smallest decision-making units, namely the individual members of the firm, that are treated as exogenous variables.

Figure 4.4 shows the basic model of decision-making by an individual p_i, and provides a starting-point for the more detailed discussion of individual codes. In this figure, p_i stands for the individual—the smallest decision-making unit in the firm—I_i is a set of information for the decisions taken by p_i, while A_i is a set of action alternatives one of which is chosen by p_i at each point of decision. The scheme includes socio-cultural factors, which influence the value system of the individual and direct his course of action. These are represented by V_i which is a set of value premises or decision codes. These factors are the basis of the following discussion.

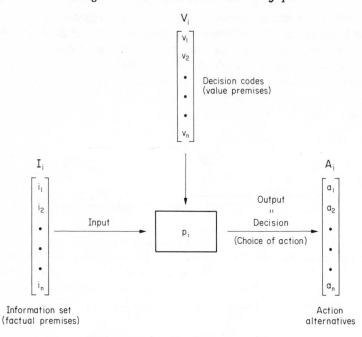

Fig. 4.4. Basic model of decision making.

Harmony based on Homogeneity

The long isolation of the country has produced a stock which has not been mixed even with that of the Koreans, an identical language, a similar way of thinking, and as a result a society with a high degree of uniformity. The more homogenous the society, the more important it is for the people to maintain harmonious relations with one another. Conspicuousness alone may cause trouble.

Paternalism and Seniority

The combination of paternalism and familyism, as well as the need for the firms to keep skilled workers and good managers when they were scarce in the early stage of development of the Japanese economy produced the lifetime employment system. This lifetime employment system resulted in long-lasting relations between unchanging members, and thus made the seniority system the most harmonious and acceptable order system with which to control organizations. Loyalty to and identification with the organization are direct results of lifetime employment.

Authoritarianism and Obedience

The Japanese demonstrate almost blind obedience to power and great respect for the superior-subordinate relation, and yet they rarely accept autocracy or dictatorship as do other Asian countries.[11] These factors become sources of formalism and pattern. "A pattern is an expected way of behaving. It is also a structure in terms of status, responsibility, available modes of action, channels of communication .... The island nature of Japan and its isolation for centuries have crystallized the patterns more than anywhere else."[12] These characteristics quite often result in merely ritual procedures, too great an observance of precedents, and a subservience which makes the people reluctant to be "the first runner".

4.3 Group Decision-making

It is safe to assume that almost all Japanese decisions in any organization are a product of group thinking, and a consensus among the group is demanded by the value system of the society. In this section the information process that lies behind the thinking will be discussed. An individual decision is understood to be a product of the individual's value systems and his knowledge. The former have already been described under the heading of "decision codes". The latter will be called simply "information". The question to be posed is that of the conditions necessary for a group to reach a consensus. Let us assume that two persons have formed a group to work together towards a common target through a division of their labour. The mentality demanding the group consensus is: "If I were you I would do the same". The necessary condition for this is that they have the same decision codes and information. Within a given organization, as has already been demonstrated, the decision codes tend

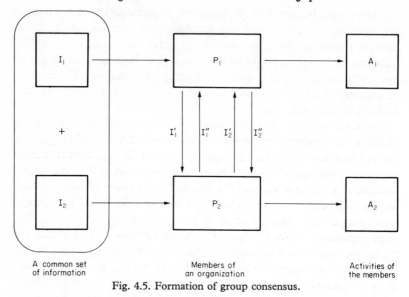

A common set of information   Members of an organization   Activities of the members

Fig. 4.5. Formation of group consensus.

to converge. This is because of lifetime employment and the natural homogeneity of the society. Accordingly it may be reasonable to think that the people in the group would arrive at the same decision if they had the same information.

Figure 4.5 shows the basic mechanism of the formation of group consensus based on the conditions described above. Here P_1 and P_2 stand for the two members of this group, who are assumed to have the same decision codes. A_1 and A_2 show their activities respectively. And the "division of labour" between them is assumed to be perfect, so that A_1 and A_2 are independent of each other. I_1 and I_2 are sets of information used by P_1 and P_2 respectively to implement A_1 and A_2. Now before P_1 makes a decision he should convey almost a complete set of his information I_1 to P_2 enough to gain his agreement and produce a consensus with him. If A_1 and A_2 are independent of one another, as we assume here, this communication route from P_1 to P_2, indicated by I_1' in the figure, is redundant. But if understanding and agreement on the part of P_2 are given to P_1 prior to an action, described by I_1'' in the figure, P_1 would not encounter any objection from P_2 upon the implementation of A_1. In this case it is likely that P_2 would give moral support or physical help to P_1. Another reason for this agreement from either side, which I_1'' and I_2'' represent in the figure, would be that the uniformity and the solidarity of the society consciously or unconsciously compel the member of a group or an organization to wish to gain an endorsement or a guarantee for his decision by the other members.

Actually, however, these two members have formed an organization which is "an organized or complex whole". Namely, A_1 and A_2 are not independent of one another. In addition, as will be explained in a later section, the division of labour is more ambiguous than in Western organizations, which naturally makes the members of Japanese organizations all the more dependent on one another. This dependence has the natural consequence of making information process from P_1 (P_2) to P_2 (P_1) more significant. Through exchanges of information P_1 and P_2 have a reasonable opportunity of acquiring the same set of information, which produces the necessary condition for them to reach a group consensus. If we do not make the assumption that the codes of the two are identical, this information process cannot be less essential for the group consensus. Indeed the necessary negotiations across different value systems will place even more emphasis on the process. In practice, of course, even in the homogeneous Japanese society individual value systems are found to differ. Where the difference is relatively great, the information exchange process becomes more subtle and delicate, and each member of the group has to manipulate information to achieve agreement with the others. As numbers grow, this process becomes more laborious and time-consuming.

Thus the consensus-forming information procedure produces huge amounts of oral and documentary information, but as a result it also produces a merit that is the full participation of the group members in the decision-making process. Once a consensus is gained, the resultant actions are extremely rapid.

Another important effect of consensus based decision-making is that the size of the group is decided mainly by the necessary conditions for reaching a consensus. In order for the group members to have as much common information as possible, the size of the group cannot be too large. The following case extracted from an OECD report might indicate this.[13]

An Example from Japan

"Our next illustration describes a state of affairs very different from the usual. It is of a Japanese firm employing about two thousand persons and recently gaining complete independence after a previous association with another. The problem sensed in the past by the new management had been not anarchy but its very opposite—over-organization and rigidity. The primary objective of the management in its efforts to develop more positive attitudes to work was to enable every worker, within his local group, to perceive his task in terms of its priorities, namely, what he was to do to help his group turn in a good performance.

"The strategies of the management to achieve this highly personal involvement ('simple yet mighty') are most fittingly expressed in this translation of their own words:

"(i) First organize a group as small as is feasible.

If a group at the base of the organization is found to be too big, reduce it to ten or less. Members of small groups can keep their independence and their individuality. Persons of different abilities, character and technical skill can and should help each other.

"(ii) Make it possible for each group to appreciate its objectives, and how they are set, so that every member sees clearly and simply what is to be done.

For the group itself set an objective which can be simply stated. Let each member then explain what this means in his own words. Turn this objective into operational targets that all members understand. After that discuss these targets and how they are to be reached, so that the group is committed to them.

"(iii) Make sure that the group has a leader. The best leader is appointed by the superior management and yet supported and trusted by the group.

Tasks of an operational kind are distributed by the leader. He does all he can to make the members aware of the need for them to be creative and original in their methods. He encourages new ideas and initiatives at all times, and promotes discussions for group problem solving.

"(iv) The results achieved by the group must be speedily rewarded and knowledge of them fed back for early appraisal.

It is essential that communication within each group should be friendly and informal. Group achievements and individual contributions should be clear to all, and it is the leader's task to provide the information making this review possible. The group must then agree on any corrective measures. An information system within the group to show progress made and progress promised always encourages members and strengthens morale.

"(v) Encourage reciprocal and dynamic discussions between the leader and his group members.

The task of the group is not only to solve specific problems or to reach routine targets; it is also to develop itself as a group and its members as individuals. In this respect the growth of the group means not only an increased mastery of the production processes, but improved understanding and acceptance by the members of each other and of the group as a setting in which to spend much of their time. Members become interested in their own development and in their contribution to all that the group decides to do.

Along these lines of small groups, and by giving new incentives, the company averaged an increase in productivity of over 15 per cent per year for four years. An analysis of this increase shows that about 5 per cent could be attributed to the small group policy alone."

This type of small group activity is best exemplified by a quality control movement called the "QC Circle", which was started in the early 1960s in Japan as a modified version of the quality control movement in the U.S. This version has made a greater success in Japan. In the U.S. it had been confined to the factory, whereas in Japan it has been enlarged to a company-wide activity in which all of the members, from the president to the shop-floor workers, must be able to participate. The key to success in the QC Circle lies in the hands of the foremen who lead a group of around 10. Therefore, the education and support of these foremen is vital.[14]

An implication of this is that if we compare the idea underlying the strategies which set limits to the size of a group with that of "span of control" in the West, we find contrasting philosophies and principles of organization. An extreme example is the Angel Industries Company, located near Kyoto, where the number of company employees is always kept under 50 because the president believes that that is the maximum number of persons that he can be able to know well and therefore manage well. Whenever the number exceeds 50 some of the members will spin out and form a subsidiary company.

With all the structural similarities of the organization chart of the Japanese firm and the Western firm, there is a basic difference. To exaggerate the difference a bit, in the latter the phrase "span of control" defines the size of grouping, and the control is from the top down; whereas in the Japanese system the need for reaching group consensus defines the size of the group, and the consensus is from the bottom to the top.

4.4 Decision-making in the Organization

Figure 4.6 shows an estimated system of seniority order and salaries of a big bank in Japan around 1968. Higher status goes with older age and higher salaries. Table 4.2 shows the age structure of the directors of the same bank. A uniqueness of the Japanese office layout is to have a large room in which employees of all levels sit at desks arranged in much the same order as the organization chart. This is illustrated by Fig. 4.7.[15] This office layout suits the requirements of an information process required to promote group consensus, as well as the Japanese mentality which is fond of team work based on collectivism. The Japanese office operates as if it were a factory to produce decisions. The information required for these decisions whether oral or on paper, is moved from desk to desk like a shuttle. If the "workers" were isolated in separate compartments, what might be called the "transportation cost" of the information would be exorbitant.

Authority-responsibility Relationships

Authority is seen here as a form of control, and the control is itself a process of influence of the behaviour of others. According to the "Acceptance Theory" authority becomes effective only when it is accepted by subordinates. And the "Principles of Management" tells us that the amount of authority is equal to that of responsibility. And authority is yielded by role setting. It was noted earlier that System P, a set of people forming the organization of the firm, does not guarantee rational partitioning of the firm's role as a whole. In other words, the boundaries of individual roles

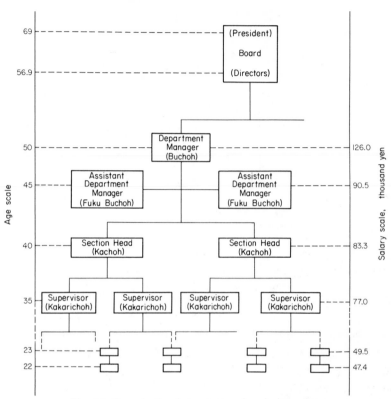

Fig. 4.6. Organizational structure and seniority order.

TABLE 4.2
Age structure of the Board

Position	Age
President	69
Director 1	61
Director 2	62
⋮	⋮
Director 32	51

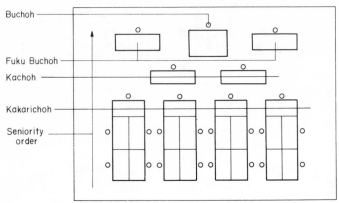

Fig. 4.7. One department in one room.

are vague or the concept of rationality itself may be different in Japan from the West.

Table 4.3 gives a clue as to the vagueness of role partition in Japanese firms. The table shows that foreign firms are more sensitive to job analysis. Figure 4.8 is a simplified illustration of this concept. Here, P_1 is superior and senior to P_2 and P_3. As is shown, the roles of the three members are overlapping one another. The activity of P_1, accordingly, is much devoted to maintaining and reinforcing the harmony of the group.

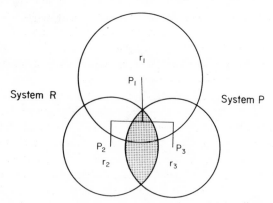

Fig. 4.8. Overlapping roles of superior and subordinates.

TABLE 4.3 *The state of job analysis in Japan*

(%)

Job Classification	Analyzed 1972 Jan.– 1972 Dec.	Before 1971 Dec.	Now analyzing	Now planning	No plan
Domestic firms					
Office	9.8	5.4	4.4	27.7	52.7
Engineering	11.3	5.9	4.5	30.4	47.8
Operating	11.2	5.6	3.5	31.0	48.7
Foreign firms					
Office	15.7	17.6	11.0	29.2	26.5
Engineering	16.4	19.1	9.0	29.0	26.6
Operating	15.4	18.2	9.5	28.5	28.5

Foreign firms are those firms doing business in Japan which employ more than 30 employees and more than 20% of whose capital are foreign.

Source: *Koyokanri no Jittai* (The Actual State of Employment Management), Rodo Horei Kyokai, Tokyo, 1974.

Control can only be effective if this harmony exists. Unique to the seniority system is the fact that not a little of the role of P_1, that is r_1 could be and actually is performed by P_2 and P_3. This means that in Japanese firms the superiors can delegate more authority to the subordinates than their counterparts in the West, given the same amount of need for control. After the delegation of this authority the superior, P_1, still holds as much control as necessary. This could be effective only under the seniority system, because seniority itself is a source of control. Figure 4.9 is an illustration of the relationship.

We assume in Fig. 4.9 that the joint sets of r_1 and r_2 and of r_1 and r_3, which are shown by the overlapping gray zones, are appropriate to r_1. And now these parts of r_1 are given to P_2 and P_3, but that much responsibility still remains in the hands of P_1. The authority can be delegated, but the seniority cannot. In the Japanese firm superiors are almost always older than their subordinates. Therefore, two kinds of authority should be distinguished. One is either potential or substantial, and the other is either formal or nominal. The former is related to the group decision-making

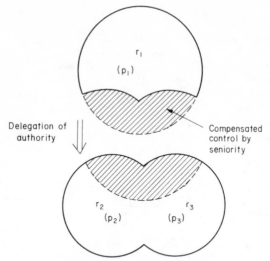

Fig. 4.9. Delegation of authority.

based on consensus. Because the roles of P_1, P_2 and P_3 are entangled with each other, the authority carries group responsibility. More confusing is the latter distinction—between the formal and nominal—which is based on seniority as well as paternalism. This carries an individual responsibility which is yet rarely activated. Sometimes a critical failure at the bottom of the firm's organization, which has no direct relationship with the top management but which might damage the reputation or the prestige of the company spirals up to the top and leads to the resignation of the president. The following words of Mr. Sejima, executive vice president of C. Itoh Co. Ltd. in 1972, exemplify this kind of authority and responsibility. "When a project fails, sanctions are not taken against those who proposed and performed it. All the responsibility for it is due to the top management who adopted it. Though rewards go downward, sanctions do not."[16]

These entangled roles and authorities and share of group responsibilities have merits as well as disadvantages. The merits include the delegation of a substantial authority which is free from complete responsibility and is protected by the superior. These merits give benefits especially to middle management.

The Role of Middle Management

Consensus before a decision is taken implies a flood of information, and much of the information that is relevant is produced at the place of implementation. Therefore, the demand for information functions to pull down the decision process towards the implementation process. While the need for the decision process to be exposed to corporate strategies pushes itself upwards. The equilibrium point of these two conflicting demands has settled down at the level of middle management. Accordingly massive manpower, man-hours and management resources have been invested in this level of activity.

Naturally, the system is only effective if the middle management are competent and know what's what and who's who in their company. In the case of Japanese firms, middle managers are well versed as regards these requirements because of the rotation from one function to another, the life-time employment and the training programmes that go with them. Thus the biggest merit of the management style of Japanese firms consists in the "participation" of the middle management in the formation of corporate strategy. The closeness of the decision-making to the implementation, illustrated in Fig. 4.10, results in a high morale and motivation among middle and lower managers. From this profitability can be expected to follow, as opposed to the situation in the West where the separation of decision-making from implementation means that morale and motivation are called for in order to promote profitability. And it would not be too exaggerated to say that middle management in Japan are the originators of "bold and active" corporate decisions because they are protected by their seniors from responsibility.

A sample is the joint venture between General Motors and Isuzu which was proposed and arranged in 1971 by two members of the middle management of C. Itoh Co. Ltd. This was one of the largest international contracts ever made by a Japanese company. As for this, Mr. Sejima, who has already been quoted, said, "These past two years our company has performed many active projects. None of them was initiated at the top. All started from the proposals of the middle management which were shown to the top in understandable forms." The philosophy of C. Itoh to make strategies, according to Mr. Sejima, is as follows:[17]

(a) Develop a strategy with objectives and form an organization to

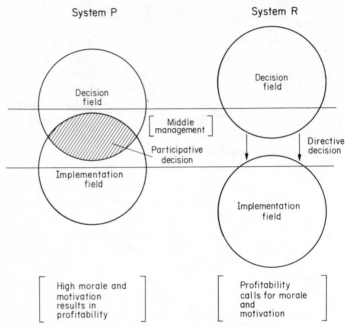

Fig. 4.10. Role of middle management.

accomplish them. At the same time, construct conditions which will help those who will be put in charge to act to the best of their ability.

(b) Most important is the consideration of human relations, therefore, complete teamwork should be attained.

(c) A consensus among and understanding of the relevant members are essential in order to obtain their conscious participation.

(d) When an idea is proposed, a decision on whether to adopt it or not should be made as soon as possible.

(e) Once a proposal is adopted, those in charge should be backed up with the necessary organization and financing.

(f) When a project is successful, the initiator and the performers should be praised and a record should be kept in the minutes.

(g) When it fails, however, sanctions are not to be taken against those who proposed and performed it. All of the responsibility lies with the top management who adopted it. Though rewards may go downward, sanctions should not.

As we saw in the Ringi system, the substantial role of the middle management in Japanese organizations has its roots in the Japanese feudal system. In addition to this, another historical fact must be taken into account and that is the purge of top management after World War II, which was mentioned earlier. This purge brought about a situation where new and younger managers in the middle levels, who did not have much experience, had to take over the management of the firms. Their lack of experience and confidence compelled them to consult with their subordinates over almost every matter. It is probable that this reinforced the role of the middle management.[18]

Notes

1. See A. Yamashiro (ed.), *Ringiteki Keiei to Ringi Seido* (*Management by Ringi and Ringi System*), Toyo Keizai, Tokyo, 1966.
2. R. Ballon (ed.), *Doing Business in Japan*, Sophia University, Tokyo, 1967, p. 163.
3. Felix Kaufmann, Decision Making—Eastern and Western Style, *Business Horizons*, December 1970, p. 1.
4. See P. F. Drucker, What we can learn from Japanese Management, *Harvard Business Review*, March-April 1971, and J. J. Holder, Jr., Decision Making by Consensus, *Business Horizons*, April 1972.
5. F. E. Kast and J. E. Rosenzweig, *Organization and Management*; *A Systems Approach*, McGraw-Hill, Inc., 1970, p. 110.
6. Quotation, translated by the author, from *Weekly Toyo Keizai*, March 4, 1972, Toyo Keizai, Tokyo.
7. Quoted from J. Lee, Where the Sounds of Company Songs Abound, *International Herald Tribune*, Thursday, March 16, 1972.
8. *Shaki Shasoku Jitsureishu* (*Examples of Articles of Incorporation*), Nihon Jitsugyo Shuppansha, Tokyo, 1976, pp. 12–17 (translated by the author.)
9. S. W. Miller and J. L. Simonetti, Culture and Management: Some Conceptual Considerations, *Management International Review*, Vol. 11, No. 6, 1971.
10. As for the theories, see, for example, O. E. Williamson, Managerial Discretion and Business Behavior, *American Economic Review*, December 1963, and R. Marris, *The Economic Theory of Managerial Capitalism*, Macmillan, 1964.
11. See Sudhir Kaskar, Authority Relations in Indian Organization, *Management International Review*, Vol. 12, No. 1, 1972, and B. S. Silberman, Bureaucratic Development and the Structure of Decision-making in Japan: 1868–1925, *The Journal of Asian Studies*, Vol. 29, 1969-70.
12. Edward de Bono, How the Japanese mind works, *The Financial Times*, Tuesday, 5 October, 1971.

13. Quoted from Report of a Management Experts' Meeting, Paris, 24th–26th May, 1971, OECD, Paris, 1972, with permission of the author, R. W. Revans.
14. See *Reports of Statistical Application Research*, Vol. 21, No. 4, December 1974, the Special Issue, Education and Training Foreman and QC Circle Leaders in Japan, Union of Japanese Scientists and Engineers, Tokyo.
15. This idea owes much to B. Hijikata, Toward Constitutional Renovation of Corporate Organizations, *Management Japan*, Tokyo, Vol. 4, No. 4, 1971.
16. and 17. All of these quotations, translated by the author, are from Anatomy of Corporate Power of C. Itoh, *Weekly Toyo Keizai*, 29 January, 1972.
18. This idea and finding was presented by Professor Y. Harasawa of Tohoku University at the Nikkei Conference held on 14th–16th of July, 1979 at Mishima, Japan.

5

Decision-making and Policy Coordination among Industries and Government

The core of management of a firm is to decide how to allocate resources "optimally" to achieve whatever aim is desired. What is to be considered next is the domain of the allocation and the controllability the firm has in the domain, taking into account the certainty preference of the business. A firm takes an action when it judges it will be profitable. The industrial groups, described in Chapter 2, for example, exist because they benefit the member companies. In the Japanese economy there are a few stages to coordinate decisions and policies of these kinds. Figure 5.1 illustrates these stages.

5.1 Intra-Group Vertical Coordination

Big parent companies exert great influence on the resource allocation of their related companies and subcontractors through their financial as well as administrative controlling power. This could be found in Table 2.10 in the case of Mitsui Toatsu Chemicals. Table 5.1 is a list of the chief related companies of Nippon Steel. The presidents of the companies marked by the asterisks were sent from the parent company, Nippon Steel. This should perhaps be control rather than coordination. According to the *Economic Journal* (October 6, 1976), Mitsubishi Heavy Industries reached an agreement with their labour union to send 110 of their workers temporarily to Sato Machines. This means that a large scale labour shift

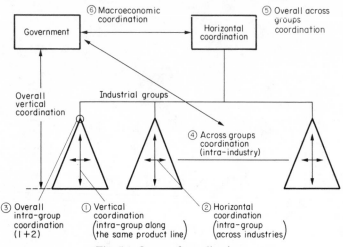

Fig. 5.1. Stages of coordination.

was planned between the two companies not through the mechanism of the labour market. Sato Machines had been helped by Mitsubishi Heavy Industries while in serious financial trouble and in the regeneration programme it found a necessity to supplement labour forces from outside. The needs of the two companies were found to meet mutually. In the beginning of 1980 this relation has developed to a merger of Sato Machines with a child company of Mitsubishi Heavy Industries, Mitsubishi Machine Sales Co., to give birth to a new company, Mitsubishi Agricultural Machines.

In 1974 Matsushita Electric temporarily sent their 2,000 employees to National (the brand name of Matsushita) chain stores, a total of 18,000 throughout the country. These stores were independent but chiefly sold Matsushita products. In doing this, Matsushita was able to digest the 15% excess in its labour forces during the recession. The company intended to overcome the crisis not by a passive strategy of lay-offs, but by a positive strategy of sales promotion to be achieved by those reinforcing troops. Those who were sent included not only factory workers but also members of indirect departments.

In this case the sales stores, though independent, are under the umbrella

TABLE 5.1 *Related companies of Nippon Steel*

Name or Company	Amount of capital (million yen)	Ratio of the stocks owned by Nippon Steel (%)	Number of directors
* Nisshin Seikoh	32,400	13.6	26 (1)**
* Osaka Seikoh	2,163	3.5	23 (4)
* Topy Kogyo	4,450	11.2	19 (3)
Tokai Kogyo	2,000	10.0	10 (2)
Daiwa Seikoh	1,500	44.9	14 (5)
Cyubu Koh-han	1,230	0.6	13 (3)
* Daitetsu Kogyo	750	42.2	12 (6)
Daidoh Seikoh	10,000	9.9	24 (3)
Mitsubishi Seikoh	4,767	1.6	21 (0)
Aichi Seikoh	4,712	13.6	14 (0)
* Tokushu Seikoh	972	54.8	10 (7)
Nippon Kinzoku	1,280	14.3	17 (1)
Takasago Tekko	1,504	17.6	17 (3)
* Daidoh Koh-han	2,250	69.9	8 (3)
Sankyo Kinzoku	1,200	14.4	17 (2)
Nichia Kogyo	500	40.0	10 (4)
Suzumoto Kinzoku	1,200	12.6	16 (3)
* Fuji Sanki Kohkan	2,000	100.0	13 (8)
Nippon Jukagaku	4,500	8.3	26 (0)
* Nippon Denko	3,030	8.0	17 (3)
Taiheiyo Kinzoku	6,600	14.2	24 (3)
Nittetsu	2,000	30.0	16 (0)
* Kurosaki Yo-gyo	2,400	52.0	15 (6)
Nippon Shokubai Kagaku	3,300	22.0	18 (1)
Seitetsu Kagaku	2,500	34.3	19 (5)
* Nittetsu Kagaku	7,006	27.1	12 (7)
Fuji Cement	1,500	55.0	11 (7)
Taihei Ko-gyo	1,800	60.8	21 (5)
Fudoh Kensetsu	1,665	22.2	18 (4)
* Hirohata Kaiun	410	100.0	10 (4)
* Nittetsu Fudohsan	500	100.0	7 (7)
Sky Almi	8,000	100.0	13 (3)
Osaka Kohzai	1,250	35.2	13 (0)
Nippon Teppan	90	66.6	12 (0)

* The president of the companies marked * has come from Nippon Steel.
** The number in the parentheses shows that of the directors from Nippon Steel.
Source: *Weekly Toyo Keizai*, Nov. 24, 1970.

of Matsushita and perhaps felt that they had gained by being so. This is an example of coordination through vertical integration.

Often this kind of coordination is found in a negative form. One example is given by the collapse of Toyo Valve, Japan's leading valve maker, in 1976. Huge accumulated debts of about 88.2 billion yen of the company to other companies jeopardized the financial condition of them, too. These debts were the second largest corporate failure in Japanese history by that time. The financial policy of Toyo Valve had been "neutral" similar to the case of Hitachi described in Chapter 2. It had had almost the same amount of loans from several banks. But the fact that it did not have a "main bank" turned out to be hazardous because none of the banks took the initiative to "take care" of it.

It is risky for a company in Japan not to have a main bank, but when it does, it usually means that the company has not only to borrow monetary resources from the bank but also management resources. This allocation of resources is another form of vertical coordination if we think of banks as dominant over manufacturers when the manufacturers are financially dependent upon the banks. In the past, quite a few bank managers have "descended" to manufacturing companies to become directors, especially since the early 1960s, when Japanese companies grew so rapidly on borrowed money. These managers were usually of the retirement age and were sent from the banks to the manufacturing companies to reduce the excess in managers in the banks' higher echelons produced by the life-time employment system. This transfer of personnel also provided an influential communication channel into the industries. More often than not the manufacturing companies were unwilling to receive the managers, however, the fear that the banks would desert them in times of financial trouble forced them to accept them. In a situation where the debt/equity ratio is as high as 80/20, as we saw in Chapter 2, failure to heed the will of the banks could endanger the existence of manufacturers. In contrast, close ties with a strong bank will enhance the credibility of the manufacturers.

In very recent years, however, during this recession banks have slightly changed their policy. They now send "aces", in addition to the "excessive" managers, to the borrowers. This recession has brought about a lot of bankruptcies, and with them the danger of causing a chain reaction of bankruptcy within the mutually dependent financial structure of "over-borrowing" companies and which would in turn lead to bankruptcy of the banks themselves. Now the banks seem accordingly to have even an intention to manage the borrowers, and for this reason they send out able managers before their retirement. Table 5.2 shows massive transfer of managers from banks to other companies.

TABLE 5.2 *"Descendent" managers from banks*

	Number of directors* who "descended" from banks	
Bank	1977	1978
Mitsui	68	70
Mitsubishi	136	156
Sumitomo	116	132
Fuji	148	140
Sanwa	83	93
DKB	182	194

* Those managers who were sent from banks and became directors in the receiving companies.
Source: *Kigyo Keiretsu Soran*, Toyo Keizai, 1979.

Of course, relations between the manufacturers and the banks should be clearly distinguished from those between the parent manufacturers and their subcontractors or related companies. But yet some manufacturers, such as Toyota, are playing the role of a bank by making loans from their retained profit to other companies. In the early 1970s, prior to the capital liberalization to a much greater degree, Toyota as well as Nissan, hastily increased their purchases of stock of their parts suppliers in order to protect their production system, based on "external production" by those companies, from the threat of take-over by foreign capital in the car manufacturing industry. The so-called "stabilization ratio", the ratio of the stock held within the network of the parent-child relationship and related companies and within the same industrial group, is much more easily increased in the Japanese stock market where the majority of the stock holders are institutions, as shown by Table 5.3. This is especially evident in the case of Toyota Motors where 226 of the parts supplying

TABLE 5.3 *Distribution of shareholders*

(%)

	1919	1950	1963	1968	1973	1978
Government & public institutions	4.5	3.2	0.2	0.3	0.3	0.2
Financial institutions	5.1	12.6	21.4	30.3	33.8	36.6
Investment trusts	—	—	9.5	1.7	1.3	2.2
Securities dealers	0.9	11.9	2.2	2.1	1.5	1.7
Other domestic corporations	15.0	11.0	17.9	21.4	27.5	26.3
Foreign corporations	—	—	1.8	2.1	2.8	2.1
Subtotal	25.5	38.7	53.0	57.9	67.2	69.1
Individuals	74.4	61.3	46.7	41.9	32.7	30.8
Foreign	—	—	0.3	0.2	0.1	0.1
Subtotal	74.4	61.3	47.0	42.1	32.8	30.9
Total	100.0	100.0	100.0	100.0	100.0	100.0

Source: *Annual of the Tokyo Stock Exchange*, 1979.

companies have formed an association (Kyoho-kai), under the guidance of Toyota, which tries to maintain close ties and mutual dependence upon the members. As a matter of fact, it is almost completely impossible for any of those parts suppliers who are located in the vicinity of Toyota Motors in the district of Toyota City to do business with Nissan. It might be boycotted in the isolated Toyota "village". This is not merely a matter of geographical distance but also of culture.

Some trading companies also finance manufacturers of the products which are exclusively handled by the companies. The typical relation of this vertical coordination of resource allocation in the form of controlling and being controlled is found between manufacturers and their sub-contractors. As we saw in Chapter 2, the dual structure in the Japanese economy has a large number of small companies most of which are to be defined as subcontractors of big companies. The subcontracting relations form several layers. Usually the relation is not contractual, but it is nearly perpetual so that it is difficult for the subcontractors to live without their dependence upon the parent company.

5.2 Intra-Group Horizontal and Overall Coordination

In 1976 and 1977, during the long-lasting recession after the "oil shock", Mitsubishi Heavy Industries shifted more than one thousand of its workers to Mitsubishi Motors Corporation with the agreement of their labour union. The latter company had a good sales of export and domestic demand and, in addition, had built a new plant in Okazaki City located in the central region of the main island of Honshu. It was, therefore, in demand of new labour forces. The shifted workers of Mitsubishi Heavy Industries were moved mostly from a dock in the southern island of Kyushu.

Another automobile manufacturer, Daihatsu Motor, announced that they would accept around 500 workers from Hitachi Shipbuilding & Engineering and Unitika (Textile). These three companies are members of Sansui-kai, the Sanwa Bank Group. In this case, Daihatsu accepted 50 workers also from Sumitomo Metal Industries. Though Sumitomo Metal is one of the parts suppliers of Daihatsu, it is quite unusual for workers to be shifted between industrial groups.

Here we must be careful not to misinterpret the circumstances of the labour shifts. Those shifted workers are, of course, not slaves. They are given alternative choices of accepting the relocation or of finding another job elsewhere. But, as we saw in Chapter 3, to move from one company to another is not usually to their advantage. For example, 405 workers of the Suwa Plant of Toyo Valve Co. voluntarily left the company in March of 1977 with the object of finding another job in another company. Toyo Valve opened the Re-employment Counsel Room to take care of them. Within a half a year 79% of them had found another job. But in the new company, the counsellors said, "They get at most two-thirds of the old wage".

This is another risk for a company not belonging to an industrial group. In the case of Mitsubishi Heavy Industries the workers could move to another company in the same group, Mitsubishi Motors, without serious disadvantage. They had only to change their residences, and when they did so, they were provided with company houses.

Resource allocation, other than human resources, also should be discussed in conjunction with overall intra-group coordination. Before we proceed to that aspect we have to note that an important consequence of vertical and horizontal coordination is that they naturally internalize the labour market and the medium products markets. Dominance of the industrial groups in the Japanese economy, therefore, may have an undesirable effect on other sectors.

On the first of February, 1973, Toshiba Cabinet Manufacturing Co. and Isezaki Cabinet Manufacturing Co. merged. Both were member companies of the Toshiba (Tokyo Shibaura Electric) Group which has 60 related companies as members. In order to strengthen the companies in the group a core organ, *Tofu-kai*, consisting of the presidents of the 60 companies was formed. The first step in rationalizing the activities or resource allocation of the group put into effect by *Tofu-kai* was this merger.

Tofu-kai has six sub-conferences for six product groups; heavy electrics, industrial electronics, consumer products, electric tubes, sales, and joint ventures with foreign companies. Each sub-conference consists of the presidents of the companies of each group. Representatives from each of these six sub-conferences often hold an executive committee to follow the two guidelines set: (1) incorporate the merits of each group and help sluggish groups; (2) coordinate opinions of all of the related companies and inform the parent company, Toshiba Electric, of them.

Toshiba had previously been a member of the Mitsui Group, but after World War II had made efforts to become independent of it. The ties between Toshiba and the group were loose. But in 1973, Toshiba decided to re-join Nimoku-Kai, or the Mitsui Group, thinking: (1) at a time when the industrial structure of Japan was changing it would be beneficial to be in an industrial group; (2) after the "oil shock" the domestic and the international economies had made a drastic change and it had become more difficult for an individual company to collect sufficient information, to secure resources and funds, and to develop new businesses.

This kind of movement is commonly found also in other industrial groups so that all of the groups have tried and are trying not to overlap activities among their member companies and to put "balanced" or optimal weight on industries concerning their resource allocation. Except for a very few companies, such as Honda and Sony, most of the big companies in Japan have some relationship with one of the industrial groups.

The more uncertain the business environment becomes, the more reasonable it is for a company to try to overcome the crisis by forming horizontal links with other companies across industry sectors. A good example of this horizontal coordination of resource allocation is to be seen in the development of nuclear energy or oil, which cannot be undertaken by an individual company. In these cases member companies of the same group usually establish joint ventures. Table 5.4 shows some of the examples.

5.3 Across Group Intra-Industry Coordination

In August of 1970, the top eight steel makers agreed to take concerted action in purchasing coal from the United States. Because of the good quality, there had been an excessive demand for it and "monopolistic" price increases accordingly. Facing this situation, the steel makers organized a special committee consisting of their managing directors to discuss not merely their competitive behaviour but also concerted and cooperative behaviour concerning the purchase of coal. In this committee the eight first agreed to make a joint countervailing power in the purchase, and secondly to accommodate any one of the members having difficulty in getting coal by selling their stock at its purchase price. The details of the actions were to be made by the middle management concerned in the companies.

Around that time the steel industry tried to establish a new policy called "orderly marketing" in their domestic and overseas sales. By then the steel industry in Japan had expanded by a series of consecutive large scale investment and, as a result, production increases. But a coal price hike and the serious slump of domestic demand brought the steel industry to a crisis consciousness and led to a change in their strategy. In accordance with their orderly marketing policy, the steel makers tried to avoid price competition in the domestic market, and to promote concerted action in determining the sales price and volume in overseas markets so as not to cause friction with steel makers of other countries. By this time, in order to decrease excessive inventory, the steel industry had already begun a "voluntary" decrease in production under the leadership of Nippon

TABLE 5.4 *Joint venture for oil development*

	(a) Mitsubishi Group Mitsubishi Petroleum Development Co., Ltd.		(b) Mitsui Group Mitsui Oil Exploration Co., Ltd.		(c) Sumitomo Group Sumitomo Petroleum Development Co., Ltd.	
	Established 1972 Paid-up Capital: ¥15,000 mil. No. of Shareholders: 29		Established: 1969 Paid-up Capital: ¥14,404 mil. No. of Shareholders: 40		Established: 1973 Paid-up Capital: ¥9,485 mil. No. of Shareholders: 42	
Shareholders	Shareholders	Shares held (%)	Shareholders	Shares held (%)	Shareholders	Shares held (%)
	Mitsubishi Corp.	24.00	Mitsui & Co.	23.54	Sumitomo Shoji	15.66
	Mitsubishi Oil	14.40	Japan Petroleum Dev. Corp.	12.22	Sumitomo Chemical	15.66
	Mitsubishi Mining & Cement	14.40	Mitsui Mining	11.06	Sumitomo Bank	7.59

Mitsubishi Heavy Inds.	14.40
Mitsubishi Bank	4.80
Mitsubishi Trust & Banking	4.80
Ryonichi Co.	4.48
Mitsubishi Petrochemical	4.48
Tokyo M. & F. Insur.	2.88
Bank of Tokyo	2.88

(Others)
Mitsubishi Electric, Mitsubishi Estate, Asahi Glass, Meiji Mutual Life Insur., Nippon Yusen, Kirin Brewery, Mitsubishi Rayon, Nikko Securities, Mitsubishi Metal, Mitsubishi Warehouse & Transp., Mitsubishi Steel, etc.

Mitsui S'bldg. & Eng'g	10.74
Mitsui Petrochemical Inds.	5.10
Mitsui Bank	4.48
Mitsui Trust & Banking	4.48
Mitsui Toatsu Chemicals	4.48
Mitsui Real Estate Dev.	2.88
Toray Inds.	3.04

(Others)
Mitsui Mutual Life Insur., Taisho M. & F. Insur., Mitsui Mining & Smelting, Kyokuto Petroleum Inds., Long-Term Credit Bank, Industrial Bank of Japan, etc.

Sumitomo Metal Inds.	7.59
Idemitsu Kosan	7.12
Sumitomo Trust & Banking	4.74
Sumitomo M. & F. Insur.	3.95
Sumitomo Heavy Inds.	3.95
Sumitomo Metal Mining	2.39
Sumitomo Mutual Life Insur.	2.77

(Others)
Sumitomo Electric Inds., Nippon Fudosan Bank, Long-Term Credit Bank, Industrial Bank of Japan, Nippon Electric, Ataka & Co., Mitsui O.S.K. Lines, Kajima Corp., Kubota Ltd., Sumitomo Cement, etc.

Source: Kigyo Keiretsu Soran, Toyo Keizai, Tokyo, 1974.

Steel and tried to regain the balance of demand and supply to stabilize the market price at a level at which they could secure a normal profit.

About a half year later this coordination moved on to yet another stage, prompted by an equipment investment plan for the coming five years. The future demand forecasts for the industry differed from company to company, and their individual investment plans were based on their own forecasts. It was at this point that the Ministry of International Trade and Industry started to intervene, or, to put it another way, started to "coordinate". The role MITI plays in this kind of situation is very subtle but influential, albeit not legislative, in the form of "administrative guidance". In this case, after negotiations the steel companies agreed in principle with the adjustment plan MITI presented. The plan was as follows: (1) The demand forecast for the coming five years was to be fixed at 150 million tons with upper and lower allowances of 5 million tons; (2) Blast furnaces controlled by this adjustment were those to be built within two years to come; (3) In order for a company to construct a blast furnace with a larger capacity than 4,000 m^3, it must put any existing furnaces of approximately 2,500 m^3 capacity out of operation. The plans should be clearly presented to MITI before the start of construction. (For more information on this "scrap & build" policy, see Section 3 of Chapter 2.)

This kind of coordination or concerted activity of an industry is more often seen during a downward trend in the business cycle, and usually first takes the form of voluntary regulation, arranged by the industry association or by a special committee consisting of representative managers from each company, and, second, of cartels which are legal in special circumstances. The details of this will be described in the next section.

5.4 Overall Across Group Coordination

Facets of the Overall Adjustments

In 1976 the Ministry of Transportation set guidelines for shipbuilding companies seriously suffering from the recession to cut their operation, and gave them administrative guidance in shaping new management policies based on it. The Ministry worried that dumping and bankruptcies might occur one after another in and after 1977 because of the growing excessive capacity of the industry.

According to the guidelines each company was "guided" to keep a level of operation which was at least not below the break-even point. The method used to reduce production, such as the regulation of temporary workers, lay-offs and the abolishment of equipment was left to each company.

In return for the operational restraint the Ministry was to take budgetary measures as follows. (1) In addition to the employment adjustment benefits applied to temporary workers, job conversion benefits were also to be applied. (2) Even regular workers, if laid-off, were to be given employment adjustment benefits, and, if fired, they were to be given job conversion benefits also.

Since this procedure may have been in violation of the Anti-Monopoly Act, a special legislative bill was considered. At any rate, in this case the initiative was taken by the Government. In the next case the move was initiated on the industry side.

In the beginning of September 1977, the Wool Spinning Industry Association decided to extend their depression cartel, which was to be terminated in October, for three more months. This policy was to be formally adopted at the presidents meeting and then presented to the government. The measures were to seal 25% of the equipment and to keep operation at a level equal to 70% of that of December 1976.

In parallel with this, the top 19 companies of the Association under the guidance of the Ministry of International Trade and Industry began to consider abolishing 18% of their equipment.

The Anti-Monopoly Act has been in effect in Japan since it was imposed by the American Occupation Authorities, and the Fair Trade Commission is the body responsible for checking restrictive practices. However, in order to obtain the benefits of both competition and cooperation, the application of the law has been amended and softened. The depression cartel is one of such relaxations, being permissible subject to certain conditions, as follows:

> There must be an extreme imbalance between supply and demand so that: the price of the commodity may eventually force companies to leave the industry; and it is impossible to remove the difficulties by rationalization. In addition, the cartel must not unduly injure the interests of the consumer and related entrepreneurs, and entry into as well as the exit from the cartel must not be unreasonably restricted.[1]

As of August 1977 there were several depression cartels in effect or taking shape in some industries and for some products. They were for small steel bars, aluminum plates, cardboard paper, plywood, cement, refined sugar and a few others.

These depression cartels may be permissible in the short-run even from a macro-economic point of view, but may be harmful in the long-run to the effect that they protect and preserve such industries that have already lost their comparative advantage, making it inefficient for the country to continue production. Namely, the formation of cartels, if justified, should be a short-term remedy. During the years after the "oil crisis", however, some industries have experienced a succession of cartels. This situation is called a "structural depression" in that the structure of such industries itself is the cause of the depression. It seems that these industries, if examined from the macro-economic point of view, should have structural changes.

On the 7th of September 1977 the aluminum section of the Industrial Structure Council resumed the meeting to discuss the structural depression of the aluminum industry, just one of the industries having a structural depression. In this meeting long-term perspectives of the industry were examined, such as a reduction in size, the forecast of future world demand, and a strategic international shift to meet demand through the establishment of a stable supply system.

The Ministry of International Trade and Industry has a large number of councils serving as advisory bodies. Many of these councils have been set up as inquiry bodies or on their own initiative to form future policies for their respective administrative areas. Their findings are reported to the Minister and the substance of such reports constitutes a very important element in planning and designing actual measures and policies. In fact, nearly all of the contents of such reports are reflected on the measures enforced by the administration of the Ministry.[2]

Legally, these councils are established as attached organizations to the Ministry under the provision of the Ministry of International Trade and Industry Establishment Law, and the membership of these councils is composed of experts in matters deliberated by the respective councils, leaders of the industrial communities concerned, general consumers, leaders of the financial community, and talents from a wide variety of social strata such as workers, educators, mass media specialists and experts from the government agencies and offices concerned.

Of all the councils the most important is the Industrial Structure Council. "This Council, in response to the inquiry of the Minister of International Trade and Industry or on questions raised at its own initiative, investigates and deliberates on long-term and basic policy related to industrial structure. In addition, it is a comprehensive deliberating organ for matters concerning decision-making on current important policies. The Council is aware of the need to formulate plans of direction for future industrial structure desirable in view of the energy and natural resources issue, the environment and pollution problem, the response to new national needs, and other similar issues. Based on this plan, the council will deliberate and study the most suitable industrial structural policy for national needs."[3]

A typical case of the council's activity has recently been found concerning the textile industry. The Japanese textile industry has been losing its comparative advantage in the last ten years. The export ratio dropped from 31.0% in 1958 to 8.9% in 1973 and to 6.7% in 1975.

In 1976 the Textile Industry Council called on the textile industry to make more efforts towards structural reform. The council report stated that scrapping of the industry's surplus equipment should be carried out strictly on the initiative of each textile firm. It requested the Government not to purchase the idle equipment but to provide low-interest business loans to small textile firms only when they scrap equipment as part of the concerted action.

The Government was also urged to eventually abolish the weaving machine registration system originally designed to restrict weavers' excessive equipment investment. It is believed that the registration system has actually dampened weavers' efforts to raise their productivity.

The report proposed that the Government should take the necessary steps to protect the domestic textile industry against rising imports in line with international rules and even change tariff rates when there was an immediate danger that rapid rises in imports of specific textile products might damage the domestic industry.

Textile exchanges should be eventually closed and, for the time being, necessary measures should be taken to prevent excessive price fluctuations at the exchanges, it added.

Many of the industry leaders previously argued that price fluctuations at the exchanges were too wild because of many speculative transactions and below-cost sales by some textile producers. They also asserted that exchanges would not be needed after completion of the proposed vertical reorganization of the nation's textile firms into several groups, each including spinners, weavers, apparel producers and retailers.

5.5 Macro-economic Coordination

So far we have seen the existing stages of coordination in the Japanese economy and the heavy role of the Government guidance for a wider range of coordination. In principle, "the role of the Government in implementing industrial policy is essentially one of persuading, facilitating and encouraging industry to move in the desired direction"[4] which is called *gyosei shido* (administrative guidance). To accomplish this, the Government, especially the Ministry of International Trade and Industry (MITI), tries to keep continuous contact and discussion with private enterprises. "While MITI officials individually keep in close touch with industry, a wide variety of discussion groups provide a continuous forum for more systematic exchanges—into consideration."[5] The general expectation for this kind of arrangement is that even the voluntary action of industry is taken on the basis of a consensus between the Government and industry.

It may seem quite natural that the mere existence of these arrangements, especially when the homogeneity of the Japanese people is taken into consideration, has given birth to the so-called "Japan, Inc." in the mind of Westerners. In order to prove the existence or non-existence of it, we will try to answer the following two questions:

(1) What share of the Japanese economy is controlled or is able to be controlled by the industrial groups ?
(2) Can the basic decision-making mechanism based on a general consensus be applied to these stages of coordination of resource allocation ?

Identifying the Power of the Industrial Groups

To answer the first question is not an easy job. A preliminary approach concerning the Big Six is shown by Table 5.5.

TABLE 5.5 *Sales share of the industrial groups* (*the Big Six*)

(%)

	(I) In all industries	(II) In the First Stock Exchange*	(III)** Of the firms attending the presidents meeting
Mitsui	2.8	18.1	11.1
Mitsubishi	2.8	15.6	11.5
Sumitomo	1.7	15.3	6.7
Sanwa	2.7	9.0	10.4
Fuyo	2.7	10.0	10.4
DKB	4.3	5.2	10.6
Total	17.0	73.2	60.7

* The First Stock Exchange includes companies whose capital is over 1,000,000,000 yen.

** Figures in Column (III) were obtained and calculated from the following two different sources, and they lack in consistency.

Source: (I) *Kigyo Keiretsu Soran*, Toyo Keizai, 1979 (II) *Keiretsu no Kenkyu*, Keizai Chosa Kyokai, Tokyo, 1979.

Here Column I shows the sales shares of the "Big Six" and their aggregation. This aggregated weight seems lighter than it really is. Considering the dual structure, it may be worth while calculating the weight of the Big Six in the First Stock Exchange which has firms of which capital is over 1,000,000,000 yen, namely big firms. The result is shown in Column II. But this seems too much. Because here, in identifying the industrial groups, in order to compile the figures a somewhat loose criterion is adopted which is made up of: (1) the number of directors sent out from the main bank, (2) the share of stocks which are mutually owned, (3) loans from the group financial institutions, and (4) historical relations. For instance, Honda Motor Co. is included in the Mitsubishi Group because the share of the stocks owned by the Mitsubishi Group companies (Mitsubishi Bank, Mitsubishi Mutual Trust and Banking, Tokio Marine and Fire Insurance) is the largest (12.5%) and a cross-listing of the board of directors is found.

In order to find the controllability of the industrial groups, we had better see the sales shares of member companies of the presidents' meeting. Column III shows those of the Big Six in the total sales of the firms of the First Stock Exchange. When we try to see the weight of the Big Six in the total economy, it is vital whether, for instance, the Mitsubishi Group includes Honda or not. In the case of Toyota Motors, though the share of the stocks owned by the Mitsui Group companies is the biggest, the Group has absolutely no influence. And Toyota has no loans from any bank. But it is included sometimes in the Mitsui Group because it is a member of the presidents' meeting of the Group.

When we calculate, however, the total weight of all of the industrial groups, it does not matter whether the Honda group and the Toyota group are included in a larger group or treated as independent. The weight is a mere aggregation of the sales of each company belonging to an industrial group. It cannot be omitted. Therefore, if we add the shares of other industrial groups to the total share of the Big Six, it may be valid to estimate that nearly one-third of the total economy has more or less controlled resource allocation. According to the newest report of the Fair Trade Commission, the status of the Big Six is such as shown by Table 5.6.

TABLE 5.6 *The Status of the Big Six* (1977)

(%)

	Total assets	Capital	Sales	Current profit	Number of employees
Big Six	24.99	19.13	15.66	26.66	6.05
All corporations	100.00	100.00	100.00	100.00	100.00

Source: A Survey on the Status of the Industrial Groups, Fair Trade Commission, 1979.

Concerning this share, data of great interest was recently reported stating that members of Japan's labour unions feel the *Zaikai* to be the most influential entity in steering the economy. *Zaikai* is a unique term used to describe the nebulous unity of big businesses. There is not any one particular organization or institution specified as *Zaikai*, which, if translated literally, stands for financial world, or, if translated freely, business community. *Zaikai*, however, may almost be replaced with Keidanren, the Federation of Economic Organizations which is a league of big business. The author's judgement is that this feeling of labour union members is equivalent to the common sense of the society. At any rate the influence ranking made by members of labour unions is as shown in Table 5.7.

These data, some of which seem too little and the others too much, do not yet draw a true picture of the industrial groups. For instance, we find a very important description about the vertical relation in the industrial groups in the report of the FTC that if we add the assets of their subsidiaries to those of the Big Six the share increases from 24.99% to 27.30%. Accordingly we have to find hidden relations there.

TABLE 5.7 *Where Japanese labourers believe the power within the society lies*

1. Keidanren (or *Zaikai*)	28.2*
2. Liberal Democratic Party (Japan's conservative political party)	27.9
3. The Cabinet	12.1
4. Big trading companies	5.8
5. Bureaucratic body	4.5
12. Labour Unions	0.4

* Figures show the ratio of the labourers who rated the items as first.
Source: *Gakushu no Hiroba*, Dec., 1979, Rohdohsha Gakushu Center, Tokyo, with modification by Japan Economic Journal.

Customary Transactions

As we have seen, the ownership share does not play such a heavy role in Japan as in the West, which is supposed to have much to do with the low ratio of internal funds vs. external funds in the financial structure which was already described in Chapter 2. What is delicate and "mysterious" concerning the relations within the industrial groups is not only the vertically channeled flow of funds and personnel but the long-lasting customary transactions. We will examine the cases of Hitachi Kiden Kogyo Co. and Shizuki Electric Co. to find such relations.

The Hitachi Kiden Kogyo Co. is a child company of Hitachi, Ltd., and 71% of the stock is owned by the parent company. Seven out of nine directors, including the president, are from the Hitachi Plant Construction Co. which is another child company of Hitachi, Ltd. Almost all of the sales are to and through the parent company, and production is planned to the orders from it. This company has 100% of the stock of its own child company, the Sankyo Pump Co. Not only from its name, but because of these circumstances, needless to say, this company is fixed in the Hitachi Group. Even its labour union is a member of the Federation of All Hitachi Labour Unions which consists of labour unions from the group companies.

The case of Shizuki Electric makes a good contrast. Although three directors out of twelve are from Mitsubishi Electric, the ownership share of the latter does not amount to a majority, being only 26%. The former, Shizuki Electric, has five related companies. For one of them, Kyushu Shizuki, it has only a minority ownership of 45%. All of the products manufactured by Kyushu Shizuki, however, are purchased by Shizuki Electric. In fact, more than 80% of the commodities purchased by Shizuki Electric are from its related companies, and four directors of Shizuki Electric are also on the board of Kyushu Shizuki. With this in mind, it may not be unreasonable to assume that the same kind of relationship is present between Shizuki Electric and Mitsubishi Electric.

Based on these clues we may be able to make the hypothesis that the higher a company in the hierarchical structure of an industrial group, the larger the dependency upon subcontracted production. The data in Table 5.8 strongly supports this.

There, the first row shows the size of firms by the (monetary) volume of sales, the second row sales per employee, and the third row the subcontracted processing cost per employee. The figures in the parentheses in the second and the third rows show indices of those sales and costs with those of the smallest class firms set at 100. As is shown, the indices grow larger because of higher productivity and value-added of the larger size firms. The fourth row shows the ratio of the subcontracted processing cost to the total processing cost. Here again we find a clearly positive correlation between the ratio of the two costs and the size of the firm, except for the two largest classes. As for these exceptions the case of Shizuki Electric perhaps gives us a clue. Even if the smallest firms, in Column I, wished to get their own subcontractors, it would be difficult, as is shown by the smallest ratio of subcontracted processing on commission.

TABLE 5.8 *Size of the firm and subcontracts*

		(I)	(II)	(III)	(IV)	(V)	(VI)	(VII)	(VIII)	(IX)
Size in sales	(Yen)	5×10^6 ~ 2×10^7	2×10^7 ~ 5×10^7	5×10^7 ~ 1×10^8	1×10^8 ~ 2.5×10^8	2.5×10^8 ~ 5×10^8	5×10^8 ~ 1×10^9	1×10^9 ~ 2×10^9	2×10^9 ~ 3×10^9	3×10^9 ~
Sales per employee (10^3¥) (month)		315	497	681	927	1,192	1,521	2,033	2,252	2,805
(index)		(100)	(158)	(216)	(294)	(378)	(483)	(645)	(715)	(890)
Subcontracted processing cost per employee (year) (10^3¥)		143	368	622	1,058	1,356	1,660	1,856	1,765	1,753
(index)		(100)	(257)	(435)	(740)	(948)	(1,161)	(1,298)	(1,234)	(1,226)
Ratio of subcontracted processing cost to total processing cost (%)		5.1	10.9	16.4	24.3	28.0	31.4	31.1	28.7	24.3

Note: Year is the term from January to December, 1978.
Source: TKC Keiei Shihyo, TKC, Tokyo, 1979.

In contrast, it would not be difficult for the big companies in Columns VIII and IX to get as many subcontractors as they wish. They have, however, technologically reliable child or related companies which can supply quality parts, therefore, it is supposed that they purchase from these suppliers rather than place orders outside for processing on commission. Accordingly, it is probable that, although the relative weight of processing on commission is less with those big companies, if the "purchasing costs" are computed, the degree of their dependence upon external production is higher than that of the middle size firms.

This reasoning may be verified by a survey on the small and medium enterprises,[6] where 70% in the industrial machinery manufacturing industry define themselves as subcontractors. Especially in car parts and household electrical equipment sectors, the ratio reaches 92% and 84% respectively, and in the recent recession, nearly 60% of the subcontractors report to have had deficits, whereas of all the independent non-subcontractors 47% reported deficits. In formulating policies to overcome the recession the independents try considerably harder to find new market opportunities than the subcontractors. The latter pays more attention to means of decreasing production costs. The same pattern is to be found in the machinery manufacturing industry for consumer products, where the ratio of the deficit-making firms is almost 62% for subcontractors and 43% for the independents.

Excessive Competition

As shown by the bantering slogan of the Mitsubishi Group, "From Noodle to Atomic Power", which is described in Chapter 2, each group tries to have every industry or to produce every product. Therefore, in accordance with the number of industrial groups, at least six big companies are counted in one industry. These six companies compete vigorously from their group spirit. Figure 5.2 shows such spirit. It would be too much to expect that all subcontractors and parts suppliers have the same kind of consciousness and pride in belonging to an industrial group but in the big companies which form the top echelon of the groups, as shown in this Figure, managers do take pride in the fact that their company is a member of an industrial group. A striking example of this is that quite

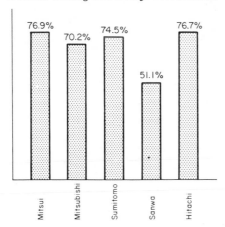

Fig. 5.2. The ratio of managers who take pride in belonging to an industrial group. Figures 5.2. and 5.3. are adopted from *Japan Economic Journal*, 22 October 1976.

a high percentage of the managers wish to buy products produced by member companies of the same group to which their company belongs (see Fig. 5.3). What is even more striking is that, in the case of the Mitsubishi Group, for example, almost 40% of the managers wish their children to get a job with a company of the same group. In 1972 the Mitsubishi Group established an organization named the "Diamond Family Club" which takes care of and promotes marriages between a male and a female in the group.[7]

This group spirit or sense of membership makes the power of a mutual holding of stocks much stronger than it actually seems. The fact that the existence of a presidents' meeting in each group brings about a common set of information necessary for general consensus enhances the potentiality of the industrial groups' integrated power. This integrated power is a driving force behind the "excessive competition" among companies in the same industry belonging to different industrial groups. The best example of this is the annual sales race between the Mitsubishi Corporation and Mitsui & Co., both of which are general trading houses. Competition such as this between two individual companies escalates into overall competition among the industrial groups, each of which, as is described in Chapter 2,

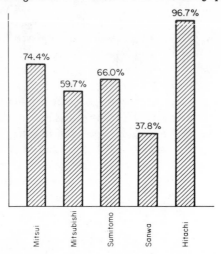

Fig. 5.3. The ratio of management who wish firstly to buy commodities produced by their member companies of the same group.

is more or less a miniature of the Japanese economy. The author believes that the biggest factor of the rapid recovery and growth of the Japanese economy especially after World War II is this vigorous inter-group competition. This competition has almost always been for volume of sales, and accordingly "sales maximization" has dominated "profit maximization" and has sometimes brought about the cut-throat competition of selling products at a price not covering the manufacturing cost.

5.6 "Japan, Inc.": Crisis Management

We have now come to the point where we can discuss whether the so-called "Japan, Inc." exists or not. In the form of a concrete organ or complex of government and industry, it does not exist. The high growth of the economy has been realized by the competition among companies and industrial groups as described earlier, and, except for a few years after the War the Japanese Government has played the role of the brake rather than the accelerator of the economy.

In his memoirs, *White House Years*, Henry Kissinger reveals that

Nixon and his administration, when they negotiated with Japan on textiles in 1969 and 1970, got annoyed and perplexed by the process of consensus formation on the Japanese side to regulate the exports of textile products to the U.S.[8] It was because the textile industry in Japan had too many companies to reach a consensus.

If we look at other industries where a few to a dozen large companies are controlling a substantial share of the market, we will find that Kissinger's remark was to the point. For instance, in recent years, with such industries as the automobile, colour TV, steel and shipbuilding, guidance by the Government, the Ministry of International Trade and Industry (MITI), to regulate exports has been put into practice. In these industries a number of firms dominate the market and therefore, it is much easier for the Government to promote or guide them towards a consensus on regulation.

The Government starts to play the role of the promoter of economic coordination when a macro-economic or a serious social impact is anticipated from a collapse of a company or an industry. Two typical cases of the former are those of Ataka & Co., which was counted among Japan's top ten trading companies, and Sasebo Heavy Industries. In the first instance, Ataka tried to expand its business to petroleum refining and invested an enormous amount into a plant to be built in Canada. However, the project collapsed because of the "oil crisis". If Ataka had gone bankrupt, it would have caused the unemployment of 20,000 employees within Ataka itself and numerous more without. In addition to this, Ataka was depending upon borrowed funds, as is usually the case with almost all Japanese companies, as we saw in Chapter 2. As a matter of fact, Ataka had accounts in more than 200 financial institutions and with its affiliates had a combined debt of about 1.7 trillion yen. Therefore, the anticipated impact upon the Japanese economy was big enough for the Ministry of Finance and the Bank of Japan to begin coordination. They asked not only the two main banks of Ataka, the Sumitomo Bank and the Kyowa Bank, but also other banks to share the burden for the national interest. Japanese banks also have fragile financial structures and have received financial assistance from the Bank of Japan. As a result they have had to accept the guidance of the Bank of Japan, which in Japanese is called *madoguchi kisei* (window guidance). This occasion was no exception. The final solution was the absorption of Ataka by C. Itoh, a larger trading company. This absorption, if we look at it in terms of sales competition, moved C. Itoh up to No. 3, following Mitsubishi Corporation and Mitsui & Co., in the sales ranking of Japanese trading companies.

For the troubled Sasebo Heavy Industries (SHI), although it is said to have been a "political rescue", the Ministry of Transportation asked the three biggest share-holders of SHI (Nippon Kokan Co., Nippon Steel and Nissho-Iwai) and the Ministry of Finance asked the main banks of SHI to help it out of a financial and managerial crisis. In June 1978, the final arrangements which resulted from these rescue operations were the efforts of the financial institutions concerned, including the Government, to give the company generous treatment and to ask the president of a smaller but successful shipbuilding company to manage SHI, with the promise of as much help as possible.

In most of the cases the actions taken are informal. Even when regulation is voluntary, the initiative is taken by the Government in various forms, including, for instance, the arrangement of meetings between the presidents of the companies concerned. The role of the Government, therefore, is more or less the promoter of those meetings. It is for this reason that coordination by the Government is easier with industries where a smaller number, usually from a few to a dozen, of firms have the controlling power. For those industries with many companies, none of which are big enough to exert control over the others or small enough to be completely controlled by others, quite often competition is too fierce for all of the companies to survive. Under these circumstances more positive action, which may be in the form of compulsory legal measures, is taken by the Government.

The essence of this would be shown by the "recession cartel" which was legalized in 1953. The number of cases permitted was 6 in the 1958 recession, 2 in 1962, 18 in 1965, 13 in 1971 and 14 in the present recession of 1979.[9] Control is applied to various aspects of business conduct. In the case of the Small Steel Bar Industry the third joint conduct of 58 companies was approved by the Fair Trade Commission and it was allowed to take the following action from the 1st of May to the 31st of August in 1977.

(1) The maximum amount of production per month by the member companies of the joint conduct was set at 520,000 tons; 380,000 tons for the domestic market and 140,000 tons for export.

(2) Each participant's maximum production volume was decided by the above volume multiplied by a certain ratio devised separately.

The justification for approval was that an unexpected decrease in exports had caused an enormous increase in inventory and that, due to the imbalance between supply and demand, the sales price had been much lower than the average cost. The Anti-Monopoly Law in Japan allows this type of cartel as a temporary emergency measure when a serious unfavourable impact upon the national economy is anticipated due to the collapse of an industry during recession. This particular industry during the long-lasting recession was given Government approval on a fourth recession cartel, an extension of the third, from the 17th of August to the 30th of September, 1977. This cartel included price control.

Repetitive recessions have hit the textile industry even harder. Measures taken, therefore, were more serious. For instance, all of the 100 companies which joined the joint conduct had to seal 30% of their equipment because of the long-lasting imbalance between supply and demand which was anticipated to continue. The average cost of production for each company had long been higher than the market price, and the amount of accumulated deficits exceeded that of total capital. This action was more serious because sealing 30% of the production capacity may have been the first step in giving up the industry to developing countries which now have a stronger comparative advantage. In fact, the Ministry of International Trade and Industry urged the industry to make basic structural changes including a concrete plan to discard a portion of its capacity. Concerning this kind of basic change Government can take a positive posture by taking the initiative.

Now if we look back at the history of the post-war economy of Japan, we first notice the queer alternate repetition of excessive competition and coordination or administrative guidance as shown by Fig. 5.4. In order for the latter to occur effectively, various factors analyzed in the previous chapters and in the previous parts of this chapter work very well.

First of all, Japan is blessed with the cultural characteristic of consensus formation necessary for effective coordination. In addition, as we saw, her industrial structure, including financial channels, can be a powerful apparatus in parallel with or integrated with this cultural characteristic for the coordination process. What is called "Japan, Inc.", then, is actually

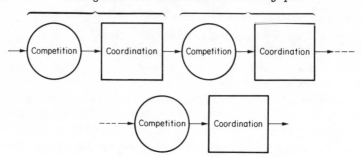

Fig. 5.4. Alternate repetition of competition and coordination.

this process in which the realm of participation is as undefined as it had been in the political world from the Tokugawa to Meiji eras when it had "the absence of a formal, clearly defined, and differentiated structure of decision-making".[10]

The process of this overall coordination is of course the process of decision-making which can, for the most part, be analyzed by the decision-making mechanism in the business organization. A vital point of Japan's overall economic coordination which differs from that of decisions in an organization is that, in the former initiatives always come from the top, but except for this, other aspects of the mechanism are the same. Especially important is the informal process in getting the informal consensus from member companies before the formal meeting starts. Therefore, as the number of companies grow, it becomes more difficult to reach consensus and the more likely the Government is to begin or is requested to begin to arrange meetings for the companies for preliminary coordination and to take compulsory measures.

Looking at the macro-economic coordination from the point of the decision-making mechanism, though the common set of information itself can be created by the process of exchanging information, the degree of the sense of "If I were you, I would do the same" depends upon how much of the same value system is shared. We saw in the vertical structure of industrial groups a vertical flow of management resources from the parent companies to their subsidiaries and related companies, and another flow from the banks to other companies. This flow is naturally thought not only to increase the ability for control among the companies but also to increase the degree of homogeneity in the value system of each company.

Then what about the human flow between the private sector and the public sector? Flow from the former to the latter takes the form of a temporary transfer. Usually younger managers, aged around thirty or so, chiefly from big companies are transferred to the Government bureau for one to three years and work there in the role of Government officers. Able elites of big banks quite often work in Japanese embassies abroad as attachés. This almost always appears in the middle management level.

The opposite flow, that is from the public sector to the private sector, is found almost always in the top layer of both sectors. For instance, the boards of the biggest five steel companies have retired high-ranking officers of the Vice Minister level, who "descended" from the Ministry of International Trade and Industry. In the petroleum industry almost fifty have descended from MITI. According to the White Paper of the Personnel Administration Agency, in 1977 a total of 198 senior officers of the Government descended to the private sector, including 32 from the Ministry of Finance to the financial sector.

This two-way stream of personnel makes a double-edged sword. It may invite corruption but it can increase the mutual understanding between the two sectors through the creation of a common value system and smooth communication channels. The fact that more than 80% of the Government officers of the highest rank are graduates of Tokyo University may have contributed to the increase in the homogeneity of the top echelon of the two sectors. But it is too erroneous to think that this flow, especially the flow from the public sector, is the major factor of "Japan, Inc.". It would also be erroneous, however, to think that this flow has no relation to the idea of "Japan, Inc.".

Our conclusion is that "Japan, Inc." exists from time to time when an overall crisis happens to an industry or to the whole economy of Japan. Various recession cartels are results of crises to the industries. The "oil crisis" was a crisis to the Japanese economy as a whole. Japan has overcome the oil crisis most successfully as a result of those controllable social economic and institutional factors.

If we pay too much attention, however, to the coordinated behaviour in and between the two sectors, we may overlook the very tough competition within the Japanese economy. "Japan, Inc." does not always exist. It should be considered rather as crisis management or, more concretely, a project team to overcome a common crisis taking advantage of the existing industrial structure. When the crisis is controlled, the team is dissolved and the tough competition is resumed. "Japan, Inc." is a special project team, rather than a construction company of the economy, with the objective of repairing the damages caused by the private sector. Without understanding this dynamism of Japan's private sector, "Japan, Inc." would still remain "mysterious".

Notes

1. See K. Bieda, *The Structure and Operation of the Japanese Economy*, John Wiley & Sons Australasia Pty. Ltd., Sydney, 1970.
2. For more details about various councils, see *MITI Handbook 1977-8*, Japan Trade & Industry Publicity, Inc., Tokyo, 1977.
3. *ibid.*, pp. 127–128.
4. & 5. *The Industrial Policy of Japan*, OECD, Paris, 1972, pp. 47 & 49.
6. See *A Survey on Reason of Existence of Small and Medium Enterprises*, Small and Medium Enterprises Research Association, Tokyo, 1978 (in Japanese).
7. *Shin Kigyo Shudan* (New Industrial Groups), *Japan Economic Journal*, 1977.
8. H. A. Kissinger, *White House Years*, Little, Brown & Company, 1979. (Japanese Translation from Shogakukan, Tokyo, 1980.) Concerning this textile problem, see also I. M. Destler, Haruhiro Fukui & Hideo Sato, *The Textile Wrangle*, Cornell University Press, 1979. (Japanese Translation from *Japan Economic Journal*, 1980.)
9. See *Annual Report of the Fair Trade Commission 1978*, Publication Office of Ministry of Finance, 1978.
10. B. S. Silberman, Bureaucratic Development and the Structure of Decision-making in Japan: 1868–1925, *The Journal of Asian Studies*, Vol. 29, 1969-70, p. 347.

6

The Changing International Environment and its Impact on Japanese Management

As we have seen, the style of management and the decision-making mechanism in Japan can be claimed to be unique. As long as they are confined to the activities within Japan, they do not cause serious problems. When they go abroad, however, they often make trouble because of their uniqueness. Here in this chapter we will examine the cause of and possible remedies to those problems and troubles which have some relevance to the mechanism and the process of decision-making in the Japanese firm.

6.1 Pressure from the International Environment

It is a natural result of Japan's growing share in the world economy that the Japanese economy has come to take into account reactions from other nations' economies. In other words, the Japanese economy has grown large enough to be an oligopolistic economy in the world. Then, theoretically speaking, not only economic but also social or organizational variables can be determinants of the performance of the economy. "Internationalization" or "multinationalization", which has recently resounded in Japan creates the problem of how the Japanese economy expands the area of its activities with direct investments while in the process of the internationally growing oligopoly. Basically, oligopoly in Japan and in the world does not bring about different problems. Namely, either overseas investment or domestic investment is a choice of an opportunity of investment.

But we can't make an equal comparison concerning the three oligopolies in the free world, U.S.A., Europe and Japan, because of their historical differences in cultural, political and economic dominance of the world. The former two have been a "majority", but Japan has been, at most, a "minority". This fact presents quite a lot of difficulty to the internationalization of Japanese businesses.

The concept of "minority" is related to the national homogeneity in Japan which has long been brewed in the geographically and culturally isolated land. In fact, almost all other cultures in the world are more or less heterogeneous to that of Japan. Under such circumstances, what kind of problems do Japanese companies have concerning international management? To facilitate the explanation we will adopt a simplified conceptual model as is shown by Fig. 6.1.

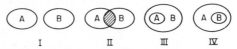

Fig. 6.1. Possibility of co-operation between heterogeneous systems

In this Figure let us suppose A and B stand for mutually heterogeneous systems which can be cultural, economic, or social, etc. Further specialization is not necessary to our logic. Here we can simply say in the case of Type IV, that cooperation of B with A is entirely possible; the cooperation of A with B is partially possible; and, vice versa in the case of Type III. In the case of Type II the cooperation between the two is partially possible as the joint set means the two systems have common cultural, social or economic factors. In the case of Type I the two systems are completely heterogeneous, and cooperation between them is impossible without a bridging device.[1]

According to Nakane, the Japanese way of thinking allows two types of relations to develop between the two heterogeneous systems.[2] One is of opposition or antagonism, and the other is that of confluence. The latter becomes possible, not by forming a cooperative body while retaining equality and individuality, but in a way that one swallows up or subordinates the other or that both completely lose their individuality in order to be united.

If we apply this concept to our model, we may well say that Type III and Type IV are equivalent to confluence, and that Type I then is equivalent to opposition. Perhaps Type II should be the "ideal typus" of Max Weber or the most common situation of international cooperative activities (including management); two heterogeneous systems having a common set of behavioral variables. But, as is often said, the Japanese system is so different from others, especially from the "majority" systems, that it may be valid to describe the situation by Type I. In this case some artificially created system is necessary to link the two completely heterogeneous systems.

Types III and IV do not exist objectively because any cultural system in the world is not a sub-system of another. Types III and IV are subjective and imaginary, existing only in the minds of people. More concretely, if we consider system B to be the Japanese system, Type IV is often exemplified by the inferiority complex the Japanese people have to Europeans and Americans, and Type III is symbolized by the arrogant attitude of the Japanese often found towards the people of developing countries. These distorted images need to be corrected as they have misled the Japanese and have led Japanese firms abroad to misconduct, inviting anti-Japanese feelings in the host countries.

The inferiority complex of the Japanese, especially of those who were born in the Meiji Era and were brought up in the years when that complex dominated society, creates two contradictory feelings. One is adoration and the other is fear or intuitive rejection. The former feeling is still to be found, for example, by the fact that almost all of the mannequins in show-windows in Japan have Western features. The latter exists especially, as aforementioned, in the minds of the older generation, who are now society's leaders, and often promotes a "cultural barrier" against Westerners. No matter how much adoration those people may have, it is difficult for them to get rid of this cultural barrier. This "plywood" complex, which was described in Chapter 1, is most typically exemplified by a case in which a man, who takes pride in being one of those leaders and in having friends in Western high society, suddenly starts to show an intuitive rejection of his daughter's wish to marry a Westerner. The true internationalization of Japanese companies led by those type of men is almost completely impossible. It should be realized that, though it is not the individuals but Japan's history that is responsible, this way of thinking is damaging to the firms and that their younger management who have the experience of a more international life are more suited to lead in international management.

The most normal situation between two heterogeneous systems in the world is Type II where they have some mutually common factors. The more common factors they have, the easier it is for them to understand each other and, therefore, to cooperate.

In Chapter 4 we gave the individual Japanese in the homogeneous country an equal value system to his colleagues in an organization, but of course it will differ to some degree from person to person and from organization to organization. As we know, this homogeneity has much to do with the lifetime employment system, which is to be seen especially among managers.

The longer a manager stays in a company, the more identification with and loyalty to it he is apt to have.[3] He is "contaminated" by the company climate. Usually, in any country, people in the higher organizational hierarchy have more vested interests in their own country, and they are reluctant to lose them even on a give-and-take contract and, therefore, often show less international flexibility than those in the lower organizational hierarchy. In Japan, managers commit themselves wholly to the company they belong to in their lifetime which is, therefore, only one means for them of getting the vested interests. In this sense, perhaps the Japanese labour climate has a much larger possibility of being accepted internationally than the management climate. One example is shown by the Y.K.K. zip fastener company.

The style of management of Y.K.K., especially labour management, is unique even in Japan where similar styles are often to be found in other companies. For instance, in almost all plants and factories of any company in Japan, factory managers wear worker's uniforms and work with the workers on the shopfloor. In Y.K.K., furthermore, all persons working in the company have only one title and that is "member". There is no classification or discrimination between managers and workers. There are members and no one else. From the experiences of Y.K.K., which operates in more than thirty countries around the world, it is observed that this style of management based upon the sense of "being the same and together" is not rejected but well received by the workers, even in countries where the people are believed to be individualistic. When we analyze this kind of response it is important to notice that everywhere in the world, workers, constituting the bottom echelon in the hierarchical order in companies, now wish to have more freedom, discretion and humanitarian treatment. If we may take this to be an inclination towards industrial democracy, the Japanese way of making decisions by consensus, with the participation of both the managers and workers, may be along that line. Concerning this, the report of the OECD quoted in Chapter 4 gives us the following analysis:

> "While it cannot be pretended that ideas introduced with such success in Japanese industry since the Second World War could be readily adopted in other countries, it is worth recalling that the psychosociological principles that underlie them have all been discovered in Europe and the United States by field research workers. What is important for Western managements to recognize is that they, too, must have personnel policies, and that in the face of the growing pressures to reconstruct Western enterprises the principles adopted by a Japanese concern can provide useful lines of guidance."[4]

But here we have to know that this "industrial democracy" has come not from a philosophy or an ideology but from a climate, which means labour management in Japan is quite often not a product of logical or scientific design. Too much emphasis is prone to be laid on informal relations. Therefore, the word "familyism", for example, should perhaps be corrected as "family-consciousness".

If we look at the management climate of the higher echelon in Japan, we will find that it couldn't be easily transplanted into other countries because of its closed character. That is, its capacity to cooperate with others in other countries seems to be less than that of the labour management. Simple evidence of this is found in Table 6.1, which shows the language barrier of Japanese managers in communicating with managers of other countries.

It is natural that the language barrier in the management level should be higher than that on the shopfloor. Workers can converse through machines in that a technical word or even a gesture can be a means of communication, but at the management level language itself is the tool of communication.

Concerning this language barrier, a manager of a ball bearing company in Japan states an interesting fact. "When we build a plant in a foreign

TABLE 6.1 *Importance of English language in doing business*

(Q) Is knowledge of the English language a prerequisite for top management in your company?

(A)   (%)

	Japanese	S.E. Asians
Yes	24	92
No	74	7

Note: "Japanese" means 356 sample managers of 300 big companies in Japan. "S.E. Asians" means 894 sample managers of big companies in South East Asian countries.

Source: Time Market Research Report No. 1796, 1973.

country, we take managers who are usually university graduates, and engineers of lower levels who are usually high school graduates. An interesting thing is that the lower-level engineers get localized much faster than the managers. The engineers learn more quickly native languages than the managers, because the managers can speak English and they try to use English no matter where they may be. So they do not learn native languages. The engineers show much more adaptability to local cultures and lives than the managers."

This seems to reinforce our theory that the higher echelon in Japanese organizations has less adaptability to or less potential for cooperating with other organizations of other countries. In other words, it seems valid to say that the international management of Japanese companies at its higher level is being practiced in a Type I situation. It needs a link to combine the Japanese management system with management systems of other countries. This may be a good reason why Japanese companies are apt to make joint ventures in host countries.

Another factor obstructing the internationalization of Japanese companies, especially in the field of management, comes directly from principles of management themselves which are not recognized by American and European companies. Japanese managers doing business in a foreign country carry the national image of Japan on their backs. Let us call this national image "national authority". We can't say yet that this authority of Japan is as highly felt in the world as that of U.S.A. or of European countries despite the present economic power of Japan. But Japanese managers in a subsidiary, in a European country for instance, stand higher in the authority hierarchy than their European subordinates. Then we find here an inversion between the two authorities, national authority and management authority. This inversion quite often obstructs the management performances of Japanese companies operating abroad, especially in the West.

In developing countries, the "national authority" of Japan is still often felt to be lower than that of European countries and of the U.S.A. This gap of felt authorities causes troubles, too. The Japanese believe and insist, after their home country has become an economic "Super-state", that their "national authority" should be felt equal to that of Europe and the U.S.A., and they behave in the company on this assumption, but the actual authority felt by the local employees is less than the Japanese expect. Under these circumstances it is reported that the Japanese managers are apt to amplify their hierarchical authority perhaps because of their unconscious wish to have the locals perceive the national authority of Japan to be as high as that of the Western countries. This behaviour, in turn, portrays the Japanese as totalitarians in the minds of the locals. These complexes, of course, make the status of the Japanese management in developing countries less advantageous than that of the West. It is indeed true that the Japanese managers doing business there may have misconducted themselves but it is also true that they have been struggling in a disadvantageous position due to the history of the West's domination of the world.

6.2 Industrial Structure and International Management

In order to study the international activities of manufacturing companies in Japan, it is of use to adopt a systems concept. A business system is, at the same time, (1) a financial system, (2) a logistic system, (3) an information system, and (4) a human system. In an organized and systematic way, in (1) money and its equivalent, in (2) materials and goods, in (3) information, and in (4) human resources, such as managers and workers, flow into the system and out. In order to grasp the international activity of Japanese manufacturers, it may be essential to study how internationally open or closed each of the four systems is. The internationalization of a company is a compound result of that of the four systems respectively.[5]

In 1976, about 38% of the stock of the Sony Corporation was owned by foreigners and in Tateishi Electric Company and Akai Electric Company, of all borrowed money, 37% and 47%, respectively, was foreign money, while in Honda 1% of the long-term credit (850 billion yen) was foreign money, and in Mitsubishi Corporation, of all the long-term credit (5,060 billion yen) a negligible 0.2% was foreign money. The latter two companies' international activities are conspicuous, but their financial systems are internationally closed. Of course, this has much to do with their capacity in the Japanese financial market which determines whether or not they have easy access to funds. The capacity of the latter two companies, however, does not seem inferior to that of the former three. This must be relative to their financial policies. With respect to this policy, Table 6.2 gives us very interesting data. This data coincides with our intuitive judgement that nationalism in the minds of Japanese managers is quite

Table 6.2 *Dealing with banks and finance companies*

In your business dealings with banks and finance companies, would you prefer to deal with:

(%)

	Japanese (356)	S.E. Asians (894)
Joint ventures of foreign/national organizations	3	21
Totally national/local organizations	66	17
Totally foreign organizations	1	11
Make no distinction as to whether the organizations are foreign or national	29	52

Source: Time Market Research Report No. 1796, 1973.

strong. In addition, because of the tight structure of industrial groups, an example of which is shown by Table 2.3 in Chapter 2, with the groups' main banks as their main financier and the trading companies as their resource and product allocator, the financial system of member companies of each industrial group is not open to diversification in its sources not only internationally but even domestically. Table 6.3 shows sources of funds for the overseas investment of Japanese companies. Here we find in all industries (with the exception of the Electrical Machinery Industry) nearly 70 to 80% of the funds for overseas investment are borrowed funds. In most cases a large share of the borrowings from "private finance institutions" is from the main bank.

With respect to this, independent medium-sized companies have much freer activities. By independent companies we mean those companies which do not belong to an industrial group and are not under the control of big businesses through subcontracts. For example, such companies as Takara Belmont, a specialized manufacturer of barber chairs which has secured almost 100% of the U.S. market and 70% of the Canadian and U.K. markets; Mayekawa, an industrial refrigerator producer having a conspicuous share of the market in the Middle and South Americas; and

TABLE 6.3 *Fund for overseas investment*

(%)

Fund source	Own fund	Borrowing from governmental finance institutions	Borrowing from private finance institutions
Mining	30.6	29.1	40.4
Textile	26.7	36.7	36.6
Iron and steel	22.7	48.4	28.9
Machinery	36.3	11.6	52.1
Electrical machinery	76.4	11.3	12.3
Precision machinery	18.1	3.9	78.0
Commerce	17.3	48.6	34.0

Source: *Wagakuni Kigyo no Kaigai Jigyo Katsudo* (Overseas Activities of Japanese Enterprises), MITI; 1976.

Eisai, a pharmaceutical company, all finance their overseas investment only with their own funds. Momoi, a fishing net maker, raises its funds in Hong Kong and Panama.

Without saying the logistic system of Japanese manufacturers spans the world. Their products are now distributed world-wide, and materials for those products are acquired from all over the world. We should notice, however, that much of the logistic activity performed is beyond the manufacturers' capacity. It is because of the existence of the Japanese trading companies. Important processes or often almost all of the overseas sales activities are performed by those trading companies. Figure 6.2 shows the ratio of all exports and imports handled by trading companies in Japan.

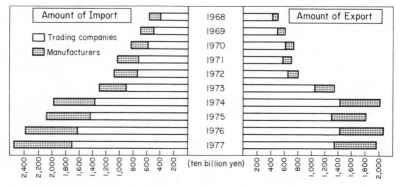

Fig. 6.2. Changes of relative weight of trading companies in export and import. *Source: Boeki Gyotai Tokei Hyo (Statistics on Trade Pattern)*, MITI, Tokyo, 1978.

There are now many companies whose export ratio exceeds 50% of their sales, but this ratio does not mean that the ratio of their own sales activities exceed 50% of their total sales activities. Namely, export activities of those manufacturers are left to trading companies.

This gives us an interesting fact. Perhaps the most common or general pattern of the internationalization activities will begin by exporting through a sales agent, then selling through the company's own sales subsidiary, and finally to setting up their own production subsidiary. If we study the internationalization process of Japanese manufacturers, however, we find quite different patterns. Quite often in their internationalization process we do not find sales subsidiaries. Immediately after the first stage, we find that a production subsidiary is set up. This is because the succeeding two stages, namely, sales by agent and sales by own sales subsidiaries, are in the hands of the trading companies usually belonging to their industrial group. In some extreme cases manufacturers are only transformers of materials imported by trading companies. Exports of those transformed materials, that is, products, are committed to the trading companies. Here manufacturers may only seem to be factories of trading companies.

In some cases salesmen engaged in sales activities abroad in subsidiaries of manufacturers are transferred from trading companies of their industrial group. What we should know here, after all, is that exports or international activities of Japanese manufacturers do not always mean their own internationalization.

Another factor which hinders the internationalization of the logistic system of Japanese manufacturers is their production system, based and relying on their related companies and subcontractors. The internal production ratio of Japanese manufacturers is quite low, as we found in Chapters 2 and 5. In the case of the automobile industry, the internal production ratio is less than 25% in monetary terms. This means, in other words, that 75% of the production of the automobile manufacturers relies on external production by the subcontractors. This relationship between the parent companies and their subcontractors is so tight and interwoven that if a manufacturer goes abroad, it would have to take quite a few subcontractors together with it.

In addition to this structural difficulty with the individual firm's internationalization, the existence of industrial groups, or more precisely speaking, the structure of the national economy itself may be the biggest obstacle to Japan's internationalization. As her set of industries is complete, her economy cannot be complementary to another economy in the world. Because of this natural structural rejection, the Japanese economy is apt to be left outside of the internationally interwoven economic order of the world.

6.3 Accumulation and Allocation of International Management Resources

As we have seen, Japanese manufacturers have internal and external factors impeding their internationalization. Some of them are historical and cultural whereas other factors are produced by their own attitudes toward internationalization and the industrial structure in Japan. The following case of the Momoi Fishing Net Manufacturing Company is a summarization of those factors.

Momoi was founded in 1905, and is now one of the biggest fishnet makers in the world, though in absolute terms its size is still medium. Momoi does not belong to any industrial group, having 150 million yen capital, 5,000 million yen annual sales and 800 employees, and it now exports 70% of its products. Entry into the fishing net industry is not difficult and around 250 such companies can be counted in Japan. The 15 biggest companies occupy 88% of the industry's exports and Momoi's export share, in particular, reaches as much as 25%. At present, the company has overseas plants in Chile, Peru, U.S.A., Taiwan, the Phillipines, Indonesia, Thailand and Tanzania. The ratio between domestic production and overseas production is almost 50 versus 50.

Momoi has a long history of overseas strategy, as the fishing industry of Japan expanded world-wide long before World War II. This expansion of fishing net manufacturers extended the business chiefly to the Japanese fishermen living abroad. After World War II Momoi first started using chemical textiles (synthetic fibers) for the nets and, as the chemical fibers do not rot even in tropical waters, Momoi could extend its business into the Southern Hemisphere. This was as early as 1951. This period was the reconstruction stage of the Japanese fishing industry and no company but Momoi was oriented to overseas demand. At that time domestic demand had not yet been saturated but Momoi foresaw the limits of its own local market. It began to find foreign markets and poured its energy into international sales.

Momoi found that the banks in Japan were inclined towards big business and were annoyed by international exchange ratio fluctuations and by government regulation of foreign investment. Momoi, therefore, built financial subsidiaries in Panama and Hong Kong. Fishing nets are industrial goods, and their use differs from one area to another and from one fish to another, therefore, fishing net manufacturers have to know in detail the needs of the users. For this reason Momoi thought that they could not rely on trading companies for sales. From the beginning of their export career, accordingly, they have not sold their products through trading companies.

This company is not well-known in Japan, and therefore, as its president says it "cannot get human resources of high quality" in Japan. Because of this, its policy is to develop native human resources in each country where they have plants. The president, Mr. Momoi, says to the author that "a good combination of Japanese and local people is best for doing good business, so we do not make any discrimination between Japanese and locals".

This case gives us not only a good summarization of but also a good insight into the background and process of internationalization of Japanese manufacturers. Expansion of activities into foreign countries is to be interpreted as the international growth of business. E. T. Penrose states in her book, *The Theory of the Growth of the Firm*,[6] that the limiting factor to the growth of the firm is management resources.[7] Simply, managers. This concept can be clearly applied to the internationalization of Japanese firms. In Section 2, we classified the possible situations Japanese firms may be placed in. No matter what situation a company is facing, it needs management skills to link or to combine heterogeneous cultural or management systems, and this management skill is acquired chiefly by learning. As we saw in the previous section, no matter how far the sales network of a company is extended in the world, as long as the sales activities are performed by trading companies, the company cannot get the learning or experience necessary to sell their products abroad. Quite often overseas subsidiaries of Japanese firms acquire their funds through the subsidiaries of the Japanese banks represented in those foreign countries. Then manufacturers do not learn how to use local funds to finance themselves abroad. In other words, the basic functions of manufacturers, namely, financing and sales, especially of exports, are often performed outside of the company and are dispersed among the members of their industrial group. Accordingly, their decision-making function is also latently dispersed within the industrial groups. Perhaps it is for these reasons that Japanese manufacturers do not have a clear policy for producing their own international management resources. The trading companies may promote the manufacturers' internationalization in the short run by providing them with export information and expedient entry into the export market, but hinder it in the long run by depriving them of direct experience. This limits the international growth of Japanese companies. Table 6.4 is evidence that the lack of management resources hinders the internationalization of Japanese companies.

An important inference we get from this is that though many Japanese manufacturers seem to have been internationalized, or though their products are sold world-wide, they do not have a mechanism to produce the international management resources necessary to integrate their businesses with the local climate, cultures and management systems. We saw in Chapter 4 that rotation of personnel within a company works very effectively, but it does not work well in international management because a manager in a foreign subsidiary is sent from the headquarters in Japan to stay only two or three years in keeping with the company rotation system. This is not long enough for him to familiarize himself with a foreign country, and therefore not long enough for him to become localized. What is a good management system in Japan is not always a good system abroad.

6.4 Internationalization towards the Inside

Though overseas investment has been greatly increasing in the past decade, as shown by Table 6.5, Japanese companies are in a difficult and delicate position concerning their overseas conducts. From the two kinds of complexes described earlier, the Japanese people believe and feel that Japan is ranked lower than the highly developed countries and higher than the less developed countries in her economic and social development.

What is seen here as a result is a hybrid of the two; protectionism and free trade. In other words, the national interest of Japan holds elements and characteristics of a developed country as well as of a developing country. This fact easily leads to inconsistencies in her attitudes towards the inflow of foreign and the outflow of domestic capital, and towards imports and exports.

On June 1, 1973, the Japan Federation of Economic Organizations (Keidanren), the Japan Chamber of Commerce and Industry, the Japan Committee for Economic Development (Keizai Doyu Kai), the Japan

TABLE 6.4 Disadvantageous management resources

	Agriculture Forestry & Fisheries		Mining		Manufacturing		Commerce	
	Big	Non-big	Big	Non-big	Big	Non-big	Big	Non-big
Nothing particular	12.5	50.0	33.3		28.2	28.3	26.9	32.8
Production technology		16.7	22.2	33.3	4.3	19.0	8.3	6.6
Sales know-how		16.7			7.1	9.7	4.3	6.6
Sales network	12.5	16.7		33.3	16.6	11.0	16.7	11.5
Management know-how	37.5	33.3	5.6		10.5	13.1	13.9	9.8
Communication know-how	25.0		11.1		13.3	7.9	12.0	13.1
Financing capacity	12.5	33.3	22.2	66.7	26.7	28.6	22.2	26.2
Human resources			27.8		34.2	32.8	36.1	31.1
Others	50.0	33.3	5.6		13.5	11.4	11.1	11.5

Big: Companies with capital equal or over 100 million yen.
Non-big: Companies with capital less than 100 million yen.
Source: *Wagakuni Kigyo no Kaigai Jigyo Katsudo* (Overseas Activities of Japanese Enterprises), MITI, 1976.

TABLE 6.5 *Trend of overseas
investment (authorized)*

Year	Total Number of cases	Amount (million dollars)
1951–1966	1,081	1,176
1967	290	275
1968	369	557
1969	544	665
1970	729	904
1971	904	858
1972	1,774	2,338
1973	3,093	3,494
1974	1,911	2,395
1975	1,591	3,280
1976	1,652	3,462
1977	1,761	2,806
1978	2,395	4,598
Total	18,814	26,809

Source: *Wagakuni Kigyo no Kaigai Jigyo Katsudo* (Overseas Activities of Japanese Enterprises), MITI, Tokyo, 1979.

Federation of Employers' Associations (Nikkeiren), and the Japan Foreign Trade Council, Inc. jointly declared "Guidelines for Investment Activities in Developing Countries". The major points and essence of the guidelines are as follows:

1. Basic Posture

   The basic posture should be such as would be welcomed by and will take firm root in the host country, and thus will ensure compatibility between the growth of the enterprise and the development of the host country. Moreover, the enterprises should aim at achieving cooperative and harmonious relations with the local economy and community in order to become an integral part of that society.

2. Promotion of Business Based on Mutual Trust

Japanese overseas investments must be consistent with the principle of the long-term interest and the prosperity of both parties, the investor and the host country, on the basis of mutual trust. Due consideration should be given to matters such as clear statement of long-range policies, establishment of sound relations between labour and management, and extension of opportunities for greater capital participation to investors of the host country at an appropriate stage.

3. Employment and Promotion

Positive efforts should be made to employ and promote the local employees of the enterprise. Due consideration should be given to the working conditions of the employees so as to ensure the health and safety of the workers.

4. Selection of Personnel for Overseas Assignment, Transfer of Authority, etc.

Appropriate orientation and training should be given to the personnel assigned to overseas subsidiary. There should be given a substantial delegation of authority and established a due length of service period to take local circumstances into account.

5. Education and Training

In order to promote the transfer of technology and skills to the host country, efforts should be made to provide opportunities for local employees to acquire them through on-the-job training or by sending them to Japan for such purposes.

6. Fostering Related Industries

In order to contribute from the long-range perspective to the establishment of the international division of labour and to the improvement of the balance of payments of the host country as well as to the development of local industry, efforts should be made to utilize to every possible extent the machinery, equipment and parts made in the host country, while extending necessary technical guidance therefor.

7. Promotion of Re-investment

In order to facilitate the development of the host country's economy, investing enterprises should endeavour to re-invest the profits of their local subsidiaries in their expansion and in the development of related industries. When remitting profits, the local subsidiary's financial position and the international balance of payments position of the host country should be fully taken into account.

8. Cooperation with Host Country's Industry

In making overseas investment, Japanese enterprises should cooperate with the industries of the host country in order to avoid concentrating in specific lines of industry and/or in specific areas and thus should prevent disturbance of the latter's economic order. In the management of the local subsidiary the commercial practices and the distribution systems of the host country should be duly respected.

9. Cooperation and Harmonization with Host Country

In order to maintain cooperation and harmonious relations with the host country, the following points should be observed:
(a) Adequate attention to the conservation of the natural environment of the host country.
(b) Full efforts to contribute to the education and welfare of the people of the host country.
(c) Harmonization with the local community of the host country.

Table 6.6 shows why Japanese companies developed their overseas activities. These activities are, as is often described by the idea of "Japan, Inc.", under the surveillance of MITI (Ministry of International Trade and Industry). MITI thought that voluntary control of overseas business conducts alone was not sufficient in order to promote the "localization" of the Japanese businesses, the key factor in carrying out effective overseas investment, and thought the Guidelines above to be only beautiful and abstract. MITI, therefore, planned in November 1974 to take action on a company-to-company basis for guiding overseas conduct.

With this administrative guidance, "MITI plans to allocate two directors or instructors to guide the Japanese companies operating abroad at the office of JETRO (the Japan External Trade Organization) which is almost a branch organization of MITI. One of the two instructors will be an officer from MITI and the other a consultant or a lawyer from the host country. Along with this, a team of MITI officers and members of industry organizations will make circuit tours of the host countries in order to reinforce this system. For overseas organizations, MITI will help to set up a Japanese Chamber of Commerce overseas for the purpose of having periodical meetings with the governments of the host countries."[8]

TABLE 6.6 Reasons of development of overseas activities

(%) Multiple answers

Reasons \ Industry	Increasing difficulty in domestic labour market	Tightening regulation for environment	Rising difficulty to secure land, water & energy	Stable supply in the long-run of natural resources	Stable security of parts & materials	Establishing strategic points for overseas sales to secure markets	Establishing strategic production points abroad	Diversification & multi-nationalization of business
Agriculture, forestry, & fishery			7.1	85.7	7.1	7.1	57.1	
Mining			4.8	95.2	9.5		14.3	
Textile	76.3	5.0	3.8	8.8	10.0	52.5	68.8	18.8
Paper & pulp		5.6	5.6	61.1	22.2	16.7	11.1	16.7
Chemistry	2.6	3.9	3.9	5.2	14.3	70.1	55.8	22.1
Ferrous & non-ferrous	23.6	7.3	10.9	27.3	12.7	47.3	29.1	14.6
Machines	18.5	2.5	1.2	1.2	3.7	84.0	42.0	12.3
Electrical machines	50.4		1.7	1.7	4.3	59.0	47.0	9.4
Transportation machines	22.2			2.2	2.2	71.1	48.9	22.2
Precision machines	44.1		2.9	2.9	2.9	55.9	41.2	14.7
Other manufacturing	31.3	3.3	3.0	9.1	9.1	55.1	42.5	15.9
Commerce	11.9	2.1	0.8	17.7	11.1	63.8	21.8	25.5

Source: *Wagakuni Kigyo no Kaigai Jigyo Katsudo* (Overseas Activities of Japanese Enterprises) MITI, 1976.

MITI, which holds strong control over Japanese industries, once advocated that Japanese joint ventures overseas should not own more than 50% of the stock, leaving the other 50% to the local shareholders, and that some industries of developed countries should be given away to less developed countries.

In March 1974 the Ministry of Finance expressed the possibility of penalties to be imposed upon those companies which performed "anti-social" behaviour by suspending financing through such governmental banks as the Japan Export-Import Bank, the Japan Development Bank, and the Fund for Overseas Economic Cooperation. The target companies, usually big businesses, largely use funds financed by these banks for plant exports and overseas investment.

As we have seen, the "Codes of Conduct" of the multinational corporation could be defined differently by the corporation itself and by the government of its country. But no matter what definition of conduct the corporation and the government may differ on, there is at least one common factor among them. That is "mutual benefit". However, this notion or concept is not only vague in practice but also difficult to define theoretically. If the financial system creates an internationally open system, namely, if there is a free flow of capital, the validity of the system is theoretically verified by the "Principle of Equalization of the Marginal Product of the Capital". Similarly, concerning logistics, a free flow of resources and products or simply free trade is supposed to increase economic welfare mutually by the "Principle of Comparative Advantage". Then what about the two remaining systems? We have not yet developed a valid theory which verifies that an open human system, with an internationally free flow of human resources yields a "mutual benefit". What then is the "mutual benefit"? It should be an increase of "satisfaction" on both sides.

With the information system, the "mutual benefit" could be an increase of mutually better understanding brought about by a freer flow of information between a subsidiary in the host country and the corporate headquarters in the home country and between managers from the home country and the workers of the host country. The need for this can be seen in the current social request for a more transparent accounting system of the multinational corporations.

As previously mentioned, "internationalization" has recently resounded not only in the business community but also throughout society in Japan.

However, this internationalization means that activities are directed out of Japan but not into Japan. What has been the focus of attention is "more overseas investment" by the financial system and "more exports" by the logistic system. Attention has not directly been given to domestic Japan. This tendency is much more conspicuous with the human system and the information system.

As we already know, of the four systems the human system of Japanese business is especially closed and heterogeneous to other systems in the world. Absolute and relative increases of local staff in Japanese overseas subsidiaries might give us the impression that they have an open human system with an internationally free flow of human resources. There is only a one-way flow of human resources (managers) from Japan to those overseas subsidiaries. The third item of the declaration of "Guidelines for Investment Activities in Developing Countries" concerning employment and promotion of local staff does not imply any possibility for them to be promoted to a post in the parent company in Japan, no matter how able they are. A foreigner living and working in Japan is always treated as a foreigner no matter how long he or she has lived in Japan, no matter how well he or she speaks Japanese and no matter how well he or she has adapted to the Japanese culture, even if he or she is married to a Japanese.

As for the information system, it is naturally closed. First of all, because the Japanese language is not an international language and because the Japanese people are not good speakers of foreign languages. Even in their own language the Japanese are not good speakers in the sense that they cannot communicate well to others what they think.

Second, as we saw before, the Japanese management skills belong to the man rather than to the system. Namely, it is more personal and subjective than it is systematic and objective. Separation of the information system and the human system is vague. An example of this is job descriptions. Usually Japanese companies do not have clearly written job descriptions and if they do, they are written in Japanese. This inexplicableness is another cause of the internationally closed information system of Japanese companies.

The third cause is the complicated information exchange system, that is the Ringi decision-making system. It is said to be a "participative" decision-making system. As a result of the closed human system, however, local managers in Japanese overseas subsidiaries have never been expected to participate in this process. The system *per se* is acceptable to the local managers. As far as the author knows,[9] after understanding the mechanism local managers do not show a rejection of the Ringi system but rather a wish for themselves to be included in the process of consensus formation.

Thus, what should be internationalized within Japanese companies is the philosophy and the style of management of their heads and bodies in Japan rather than their hands and legs stretched overseas. "Internationalization" is needed to be directed towards the inside of Japan.

Notes

1. Naoto Sasaki, An Exploration of Internationalization of the Japanese Management, *Chuo Koron Keiei Mondai*, Chuo Koron, Tokyo, Spring, 1973 (in Japanese).
2. Chie Nakane, *Conditions of Adaptation*, Kodansha, Tokyo 1973 (in Japanese). See also, Chie Nakane, *Japanese Society*, Penguin Books Ltd., 1974.
3. See James G. March and Herbert A. Simon, *Organizations*, John Wiley & Sons, Inc., 1958.
4. The same source as Note 13, Chapter 4, p. 17.
5. Naoto Sasaki, Characteristics of Internationalization of the Japanese Management, *Chuo Koron Keiei Mondai*, Chuo Koron, Tokyo, Winter, 1975 (in Japanese). See also, Naoto Sasaki Internationalization of the Japanese Companies, in *Conference: Japanese Economy*, Tokyo University Press, Tokyo, 1976 (in Japanese).
6. Edith T. Penrose, *The Theory of the Growth of the Firm*, Basil Blackwell & Mott Ltd., 1959.
7. Concerning this, see Ryutaro Komiya, *Gendai Nihon Keizai Kenkyu (A Study on the Present State of the Japanese Economy)*, Tokyo University Press, Tokyo, 1975, pp. 212–214 (in Japanese).
8. These quotations are adopted from articles of the *Japan Economic Journal* (a newspaper).
9. These five years the author has been the planning advisor and program co-ordinator of an international seminar, Program for Cross Cultural Management, sponsored by the Association for Overseas Technical Scholarship in Tokyo, which is chiefly for local managers of developing countries working for Japanese companies. So far we had around 150 participants from more than 20 countries. In the past programmes the Japanese decision-making system was well understood, and the participative characteristics of it even appealed to the participants.

7

Present Drastic Changes
Towards a Collapse?

It is very unlikely that a national character and a culture will change drastically within a decade. Although the Japanese people are said to be becoming more and more individualistic, according to a survey made by the Japan Broadcasting Corporation[1] more than 70% of the Japanese still wish to have as their business partner a person with more sociability and less ability than a person with little sociability and more ability. The majority of them still prefer an all-round relationship, including both official and private aspects, with their colleagues at work. Another survey by the same corporation tells us that nearly 85% of the Japanese under thirty believe that job-hopping would degrade their social value.[2] It is now pervasive that the merit system is increasing its share in the wage and salary scale, based on the seniority order. The weight of the seniority system, therefore, is gradually decreasing in the Japanese society but loyalty to and identification with the organization do not show symptoms of diminishing. Accordingly, the organizational climate will possibly remain as it has been into the foreseeable future.

Other aspects of Japan's business conduct, which have been described earlier, are not likely to change drastically either. For instance, the industrial groups are strengthening their ties by increasing mutually held stocks. Especially during the present energy crisis each industrial group is searching for oil and coal sources with the joint efforts of member companies and such activities will probably be coordinated by the Government. Somehow or another the internationalization of the Japanese economy and of individual companies will be advanced by external pressures from abroad and by their own domestic needs, which in turn will change the structure of the economy. The last stage of this internationalization, however, for most of the companies will be to change the core of the corporate body.

Up until a few years ago, especially prior to the oil crisis, the Japanese society had anticipated that companies would have to face changes caused by the incoming younger generation who were thought to be selfish and apathetic with no interest in organizational goals and "spoiled by the over-care in the nuclear family, the hard and severe race to enter good universities and growing economic welfare". But, surprisingly, a critically drastic and "dangerous" change has come about not from the bottom of the seniority order organization but from the upper echelon, higher than the middle management level. This change is what is called the "Retirement Age Revolution".

Marubeni (trading company) started a new retirement system in 1980 having three possible alternatives: (1) to retire at the age of 55; (2) to retire at the age of 50 receiving a retirement allowance and being re-employed as a special staff member up until the age of 60 with the level of salary kept at 80% of that at retirement time; and (3) to retire at the age of 50 with a special retirement allowance which is calculated by using the same multiplying parameter as that used at the age of 55. Retirement at the age of 55 had been the most common practice up until a few years ago, so that option (1) follows that pattern which is considered to be for the "selected" or elite. The other two options could be interpreted as devices to reduce redundant management resources. This type of optional retirement system has been becoming more and more prevalent and the age at which the optional system begins is earlier in some companies, such as Kanebo at the age of 45, Showa Denko Chemical at the age of 40 and Mitsubishi Rayon at the age of 35.[3]

As we have seen, the lifetime employment system and the seniority system have long been believed to be cultural systems not only by foreigners but also by the Japanese themselves. These two systems with the company-wide labour unions have supported the rapid growth of the Japanese economy after World War II, and the very managers and workers who have borne the burden of achieving Japan's growth are now facing this threat. At the point where they have made their society rich, that very society has begun to get rid of them. Behind this there is a strong economic reason which is the slowdown of economic growth in recent years.

The Japanese management based upon those cultural factors has been a management for growth. It works best and most effectively during periods of growth. Simple arithmetic easily verifies that under the seniority wage system the higher the growth rate the lower the unit labour cost.[4]

But when the economy has reached a slowdown or the near saturation level, to make matters worse, the age structure of the society has changed from a pyramidal one with a broad base to a trapezoidal one with a much broader ceiling. This tendency naturally pushes up the companies' labour costs (including salaries) to an unbearable level. This would be easily understood if we look at Japan's population data which states that the population structure has become almost the same as that of the highly developed countries of the West and, while in the West the wage index of the older workers over 45 to that of younger workers (aged 20 through 24) is between 100 and 115, in Japan it is over 150.[5] This anticipated fear of saturating demand and the creeping supply cost increases has made it almost a fashion especially among big business to adopt the optional retirement system.[6] Though it says "optional", quite often the system is compulsory given in the form of a recommendation or advice. As we saw in Chapter 3, to move from one company to another is unfavourable in Japan, and the degree increases as the employee gets older. Before the birth of a society which gives citizenship and equality to "job-hoppers", to promote an early retirement age is almost a cruel threat. Especially managers, whose position is higher than Ka-cho, are victims of this threat because by law they cannot be members of the labour unions and, therefore, are defence-less. Lifetime employment could be viewed as a utopia where employees have "employees sovereignty"—much like the consumer's sovereignty—by which they choose a company to stay with. It should be the best company from every possible viewpoint which makes the employees want to stay for a lifetime. This utopia seems to have become just an "impossible dream".

On the other hand, while this "purge" is storming, a counter-measure is being taken by the labour unions and that is to try to force the companies to extend the retirement age to 60 years of age. With or without the pressure, as of the beginning of 1980, roughly one-third of the companies have introduced the new retirement age. However, it has brought about a trade-off between employment security and economic loss as a compromise to the labour unions. This economic loss is in the form of levelling wages after the age of 50.

This change gives a much more serious impact to the wage system as a whole than it seems. Because it is not related to the seniority system, it supports the general tendency of the wage system towards a merit system. Already it has become prevalent in the business community in Japan to separate the promotion system and the wage or salary system. Among big business almost 80% and among the smaller companies more than 60% of all companies have this separation. Under this system a scale of ability grades and a classification of work and jobs are made respectively. Promotion in the official post ranking and that in the ability grade scale are two different things. Accordingly, it can occur that an immediate subordinate earns more than his superior.

As aforementioned, it is true that younger generations are changing but, because of growing uniformity in the generations, it is unlikely that they will lose their group-consciousness. At least, however, one thing is indisputable and that is that they are losing their identification with the companies they are working for. We already know that the past growth of the economy owes much to the dedication of the middle management in the private companies but they are now losing their sense of security and have a bleak future.

In the long-run cultural changes brought about by the influx of the younger generation from the bottom of organizations will be dominant. At present economic interests on the part of the company are overwhelming traditional cultural factors in the mind of employees and managers of the higher echelon. So far the climate in the Japanese management has held positive profit sharing exemplified by bonuses and negative profit (loss) sharing in the way to decrease together receipts from the company. Now it is losing at least the latter.

These changes may weaken the dynamism of Japanese companies and may lead to a total collapse. They are destroying themselves. There is a chance, however, that they may make an "Aufheben" from those conflicting elements, namely a better combination of Japanese ethos and Western logos. The present situation may be simply a transition period to that new stage.

Notes

1. *Gendai Nihonjin no Ishiki Kozo* (Structure of Consciousness of Modern Japanese), The Japan Broadcasting Corporation Press, Tokyo, 1979.

2. *Nihonjin no Shokugyokan* (Japanese View of Vocation), The Japan Broadcasting Corporation Press, Tokyo, 1979.
3. *Weekly Gendai*, 23 August 1979, Kodansha, Tokyo.
4. See Kang Chao, Labour Institutions in Japan and Her Economic Growth, *The Journal of Asian Studies*, Vol. 28, 1968/69.
5. *The Economic Journal*, 19 August 1979, Tokyo.
6. For small and medium enterprises it has already long been common to have a seniority wage system which has its peak at around the age of 40.

Index